MW00812815

GOLDEN NUGGETS

FROM GOD'S WORD

Jennifer,
I pray you'll be
blessed as you read
God's Golden Nuggets!
Merry Christmas 2023!
Nancy White

Copyright © 2022 by Nancy White

Published by Kudu Publishing

All rights reserved. No portion of this book may be reproduced, stored in a retrieval system, or transmitted in any form or by any means—electronic, mechanical, photocopy, recording, scanning, or other—except for brief quotations in critical reviews or articles, without prior written permission of the author.

Unless otherwise marked, scripture quotations are taken from the King James Version of the Bible. Public domain. | Scripture quotations marked NKJV are taken from the New King James Version®. Copyright © 1982 by Thomas Nelson. Used by permission. All rights reserved.

For foreign and subsidiary rights, contact the author.

Cover design by: Sara Young

ISBN: 978-1-959095-22-4   1 2 3 4 5 6 7 8 9 10

Printed in the United States of America

100 DAY DEVOTIONAL
TO ENRICH YOUR LIFE

GOLDEN NUGGETS

FROM GOD'S WORD

NANCY WHITE

KUDU
PUBLISHING

CONTENTS

ACKNOWLEDGMENTS

I would like to give a gigantic thanks to my husband and family, who continually helped me through the process of getting this book written and published. Your love, patience, encouraging words, and constructive help enabled me to see past the daunting tasks at hand and kept me moving forward.

I want to give a special shout out and big thank you to all who encouraged me during my initial Facebook inspirational pieces, but especially to Debbie, Ridge, Nancy, Joanna, and Victoria. There were so many others who reassured me along the way, but those five truly ignited the fire in me that brought this book to fruition.

Words fail me in describing my other friends (I would like to name you all, but I don't want to leave anyone out by accident) along the way who have inspired me, encouraged me, and counseled me when I dealt with insecurity in doing this. I knew God had put it on my heart to write this book, but like Moses, I could only think of the impossibilities in myself and my inabilities. My friends continually reminded me that this was God's book, so I needed to let Him do what only He could do.

THANK YOU ALL FOR BELIEVING IN ME AND THIS BOOK! Thank you for loving me unconditionally and seeing more in me than I saw in myself.

INTRODUCTION

T he Nancy White Interpretation (NWI) came to fruition years ago because of my desire to better understand what God's Word says. Even though there are many wonderful translations of the Bible, the one that I most often use is the King James Version. Since I was given that translation as a youth, it was the one that I grew to love. Even though I have a general understanding of what I read, I sometimes find certain words or verses are not as clear to me. It is because of that lack of clarity that I began searching for answers to my questions.

A former Bible study teacher introduced me to a tool she used called the "Strong's Exhaustive Concordance of the Bible" written by an American theologian named James Strong. He wrote it as "a thorough verbal index to the Holy Scriptures"[1], and for "showing every word of the text of the common English version of the canonical books, and every occurrence of each word in regular order; together with dictionaries of the Hebrew and Greek words of the original, with references to the English words"[2] (title page). In other words, you look up any word in the Bible, exactly how it is spelled. The Strong's Concordance lists every single word in the Bible, in every verse it is located. After you find the word you are looking for (in alphabetical order), you then look for the book, chapter, and verse from the Bible that you are searching for and it will give you a corresponding number that is assigned to that specific word in that specific verse. The back of the Concordance is divided into two sections, Hebrew for Old Testament references and Greek for New Testament references. Once you have found the number associated with the Hebrew or Greek word you are trying to locate, it will give you the definitions of the word.

I have discovered that by using this tool, many scriptures literally have come to life with clarity and sometimes have even produced those 'aha' moments by which the Lord was able to show me some deeper understandings. Occasionally, the words mean exactly what I thought or knew. Other times, the definitions changed my perception as to what I had previously known or thought I knew.

Listed below are three examples of definitions that gave me new insight:

1. SAVED—1 Timothy 2:4 states, "Who will have all men to be saved, and to come unto the knowledge of the truth."

---

1 Strong, James. *The New Strong's Expanded Exhaustive Concordance of the Bible.* Red letter ed. Nashville, Tenn.: Thomas Nelson, 2010.

2 ibid

"Greek #4982- Sozo- to save, i.e. deliver or protect (lit. or fig.) heal, preserve, save(self), do well, be (make) whole."[3]

So, the NWI might say, "Who will have all men to be saved, delivered, protected, healed, and made whole." God's desire is for my good and this displays the fullness of what our loving Father wants for us.

2. Peace—In John 14:27a, Jesus declares, "Peace I leave with you, not as the world giveth, give I unto you."

"Greek #1515- i-ray'-nay- prob. from a primary verb eiro (to join): peace (lit. or fig.) by impl. prosperity: one, peace, quietness, rest, +set at one again."[4]

The NWI might read, "Rest, peace, and being set at one again I leave you: not as the world gives." This changes my perception of what I previously understood peace to mean based on the way society refers to it, as opposed to what God intends it to mean. Now I see that Jesus wants me to have more than just peace and rest, which was my basic understanding. He also wants me to "be set at one again" and not be all over the place, confused, scattered, and stressed.

3. GRACIOUS—In this familiar portion of the blessing that many pastors speak over their congregation, Numbers 6:25 says, "The Lord make his face shine upon thee, and be gracious unto thee."

"Greek #2603- khaw-nan'- to bend or stoop in kindness to an inferior; to favor, bestow, to implore (i.e. move to favor by petition), beseech, x fair, (be, find, shew) favour (able), be (deal, give, grant, (gracious (-ly), intreat, (be) merciful, have (shew) mercy (on, upon), have pity upon, pray, make supplication."[5]

The NWI might state: "The Lord make His face shine on you and be moved with favor towards you, be merciful to you, have pity on you and be moved with kindness to you." To me, this more clearly illustrates the great love of the Father to us His beloved children.

Typically, I look up all of the keywords in the verses, which obviously takes time, but the reward is a clearer picture of what the Lord intended us to see in His Word. It was because of my study of God's Word, trying to dig deeper by utilizing the Strong's Concordance and other resources, to get more clarity and understanding, that the Lord gave me His "Golden Nuggets". He wants us to find them so that we can discover His promises and be enveloped in His love, so that we might better understand what He has provided for us through His Son, Jesus.

If you are interested in using the Strong's Concordance to help you study the Bible, it can be found in book form or as an app. There are other translations for it as well if you don't enjoy the King James Version. I enjoy using both. I pray that if you choose to utilize this Bible study tool, God will open up your eyes to see more of Who He is and what all He has done for you, as well as reveal those "Golden Nuggets" from God's Word.

---

3 ibid

4 Strong, James. *The New Strong's Expanded Exhaustive Concordance of the Bible.* Red letter ed. Nashville, Tenn.: Thomas Nelson, 2010.

5 ibid

DAY 1
JOY

PSALM 119:143

"Trouble and anguish have taken hold on me: yet
thy commandments are my delights."

*"Adversity, affliction, anguish, distress, sorrow, and
tribulation have occurred to me; your commandments
and precepts are my delight and pleasure." (NWI)*

God's Word brings us pleasure and delight, even when—and probably especially when—we are in the midst of problems. No matter what comes our way, we can have joy in the middle of it. Even when we are sad, hurt, sick, grieving, going through personal, physical, financial, family, or work issues, we can still have God's peace and joy. Our joy is not dependent on everything in our life being good or perfect.

Having joy is a decision to trust God and His Word, believing He can perform the impossible—no matter the circumstances—and resting in that decision. It is knowing that, even if things don't go the way we want, He has all things under control and will ultimately "work it together for our good" (Romans 8:28). It's the quiet confidence that "God's got this," no matter what the doctor says, what the budget says, what is happening around us, or who has hurt us. As we read God's Word, it builds our faith and enables us to think beyond what we can see, hear, or feel. God's Word settles our spirit, fears, and anxieties and brings peace, joy, hope, faith, and encouragement.

The psalmist states that God's commandments are his delights. When I think of something that delights me, I think of things that are beautiful or personal like family, mountains, rainbows, oceans, flowers, babies, friends, and other such things that bring me excitement and joy. But shouldn't we be so intimate with the Lord that His commandments (His Word) bring us joy and excitement? After all, through God's Word, we learn about Jesus, His love for us, His salvation, His healing, His deliverance, His peace, His freedom, His wisdom, and so much more. It's through God's commandments that we learn what pleases Him, and what is or isn't best for us. So yes, we should be like the psalmist, able to say that even though we are going through difficult times, it is God's Word that delights us, brings us hope, gives us peace, and gives us joy to sustain us.

> Lord, I pray that no matter what comes my way, I will put my trust in You. As I read Your Word, it will help me to continue in Your peace and it will bring me joy. During my troubles and problems, I choose to be happy and to trust You. I choose to delight myself in You and Your Word.

MY REFLECTION:

_____

_____

_____

_____

_____

_____

_____

_____

_____

_____

_____

_____

_____

_____

_____

_____

_____

_____

_____

_____

_____

_____

DAY 2
SEARCHING OUT

EZEKIEL 34:16a

"I will seek that which was lost, and bring again that
which was driven away, and will bind up that which was
broken, and will strengthen that which was sick."

*"I will search out, by any method, strive after, and desire the one which
has wandered away, lost themselves, and cannot escape, and I will
fetch home again, refresh, relieve, rescue, and restore the one who
is cast down, stricken, drawn away, misled, and withdrawn, and I will
bind up and wrap about the broken-hearted, crushed, and destroyed,
and I will strengthen, cure, help, repair, mend, and encourage the
one who is weak, sick, afflicted, grieved, and wounded." (NWI)*

This is the Lord speaking to Ezekiel the prophet, telling him to prophesy against the shepherds of Israel. In the beginning of chapter 34, the Lord is scolding the shepherds (pastors) for not tending to their sheep by feeding them, not taking care of those who were sick, or for allowing the sheep to be scattered. In verse 11, the Lord tells Ezekiel that He will "search my sheep and seek them out." In verse 12, the Lord says that He will "deliver them out of all places where they have been scattered in the cloudy and dark day." He continues in verses 13 to 15 to describe how He will take care of His scattered sheep. In verse 16, we see God's fatherly, caring, loving and compassionate heart for His "sheep" (children).

If you have ever lost your child somewhere, you have a better understanding of what the Lord is saying in verse 16. I remember losing one of my sons when he was about six at a local amusement park for about five minutes. It seems like hours, because the panic that comes into your heart is overwhelming. When one of God's children gets "lost" spiritually, the Lord will do anything it takes to find him—just like I did that day, looking everywhere I could, asking everyone I saw.

But you might wonder, *How does this apply to me?* I hope I'm not the only one who has lost my way over the course of my life. There are various reasons this can occur. It could be that you had a pastor leave the church—and the body of believers there—to "fend for themselves." This happened in a church I was a part of, and it brought havoc to many of the people that attended there until things were addressed. Your children could get way off-track and away from the Lord. Your heart could be broken because of something that happened, causing you to question the Lord. Someone you love may have died too early because of sickness or an accident, which brings many people into deep depression. You may have been physically or sexually abused and feel betrayed by that person—which could also lead you to feeling betrayed by the Lord. There are so many scenarios that can cause us to stray from the Lord like my son strayed from us while at the park. No matter what it was that causes someone to veer off from following the Lord, it grieves His heart.

Look how diligently He will search for and help us—by any method. He'll go after those that have gone astray and can't seem to find a way to escape. He'll bring them back. He'll rescue and restore them. He'll comfort those who are broken-hearted and crushed. He'll strengthen, mend, and encourage their grief, sickness, and wounds. Notice also that, in this passage, God isn't judging them or criticizing them; instead, He's trying to bring them back to where they need to be: with Him. He wants His children to be whole, healthy, content, and blessed, not broken and downtrodden.

> Father, thank You for Your love towards me. Thank You that I am never so far away from You that You can't find me. Thank You that You will do whatever it takes to bring me back to You. Thank You, Lord, for Your mercy, grace, compassion, healing, and peace.

MY REFLECTION:

_____

_____

_____

_____

_____

_____

_____

_____

DAY 3
POWER

I CORINTHIANS 4:20
"For the kingdom of God is not in word, but in power."

"For the royalty, realm, reign, and kingdom of God is not in something said or thought, it's not in reasoning or motive, it's not in fame, intent, or preaching, and it's not in works, but in the miraculous power, strength, and mighty wonderful works of the Lord." (NWI)

When God speaks, things happen. In Genesis, He spoke, and the world was created. When Jesus spoke, people were healed and delivered, and the raging waters were calmed and stilled. God's kingdom deals with the supernatural, with miracles, with "mighty wonderful works." When the Israelites were confronted with the Red Sea, God told Moses to hold up his rod; when he did, the Red Sea parted so that millions of people were able to cross through it on dry ground. When Daniel was thrown into the lion's den because he publicly prayed, God shut up the mouths of the lions so that he wasn't touched at all. When Shadrach, Meshach, and Abednego were thrown into a burning fiery furnace seven times hotter than normal—where even the people throwing them from the outside were burned—those three didn't even have on them the smell of smoke!

Miracles are recorded throughout the Old and New Testaments, and yet today, many aren't seeing any occur. Why? People in other parts of the world are seeing regular miracles: healings, the dead brought back to life, and salvations by the thousands. But why aren't we seeing them?

I wonder if it has anything to do with our "works over faith" mentality, or maybe our obsession with the heroes of the entertainment and athletic world, or the way we watch and listen to every Christian preacher, singing group, or evangelist—even, at times, our own understanding—rather than having simple faith in the Lord and trusting Him to fulfill His Word.

I love the lyrics, "There is power, power, wonder-working power in the blood of the Lamb." Are our eyes on Him, or are they elsewhere? If we will simply believe God and His Word, trust Him, and not look to other things or people—not try to figure it all out ourselves—we will see more of the power that we read about in the Bible—the power that others are experiencing.

Lord, I come to You in the name of Jesus, asking You to help me to always seek You and Your kingdom. Help me to have eyes to see what You are doing all around me daily, that I may give You the glory due Your name.

MY REFLECTION:

_____

_____

_____

_____

_____

_____

_____

_____

_____

_____

_____

_____

_____

_____

_____

_____

_____

_____

_____

_____

_____

_____

DAY 4
HOPE

PSALM 130:5

"I wait for the Lord, my soul doth wait, and in his word do I hope."

"I expect and patiently wait for the Eternal Lord, my desires, heart, mind, and soul patiently wait, and in His word, glory, power, promise, provision, purpose, and work do I hope and trust." (NWI)

This verse clearly defines how we should live. Our whole being—mind, heart, desires, and soul—should patiently trust God to fulfill His Word in our lives. We should expect God's glory, power, and provision to be actively working in our lives. We must have hope and trust in Him for all of our needs to be met.

Unfortunately, we most often want those needs met yesterday. But our faith is exercised and grown when we put our hope and trust in Him and then patiently wait for His answers. Our desires are always pressing on us to want more now—to want God to act now—to demand that He change things now. Sometimes, that's exactly what God does: He answers us immediately. More often than not, though, our answers are delayed. They are God's way of seeing if we are actually patiently trusting Him, or if we're just going through the motions of praying to get what we want.

Are we going to continue to do what He last instructed us to do? Are we holding onto His promises? Are we living for Him even when we're going through trials? Are we reading His Word and praising Him for His goodness to us? In other words, are we waiting patiently for the answers while we go about our business, believing God to do what He needs to do in, for, and through us?

It reminds me of a story in which a child asks his father for a marshmallow. The father tells the young boy that he can't have it now. His little son repeatedly asks, begs, and even cries to get his marshmallow, but the dad continues to tell the son, "Not now." What the little boy doesn't realize is that the father has a bigger plan already figured out to roast hot dogs and marshmallows around their fire pit for dinner. The young child can't see past his own immediate desire to have a marshmallow, so he can't realize that there is about to be something so much better than he can figure out himself.

That is how God works with us, as well. We want what we want when we want it, but God may not be allowing us to have what we want right now. It's not that He doesn't intend on letting us have our desires; it could be that He has something bigger and better in mind (beyond what we could ask or think). We may not be able to see all God has planned for us, so it is our job to trust Him and wait for Him to bring His answers when He sees that it is the right timing.

In the example above, the little boy only had to wait a few hours; but sometimes, the answer may not come that quickly. There may be reasons, of which we are unaware, that require more time to pass first. For example, it may seem, when we are 14 and driving the golf cart around, that we are ready for our driver's license; but we all know there is a lot more involved in driving a car than a golf cart. And yet many teenagers probably feel completely adequate. So the parent must wait until the teenager is old enough, responsible enough, has learned all of the rules, and has taken the driving test before the young person is able to own and drive a car.

God understands this principle much better than we ever could. When we are asking Him for something, He may be keenly aware of things we need to learn and grow in so that we are able to have our desired request. It's not that God doesn't hear us or want to bless us—it's that we still have some things to learn before the prayer can be answered.

Lord, teach me how to wait patiently on You. Show me how to trust Your timing and how to not try to get ahead of what You need and want to do in me. You have a purpose and plan for my life, and You will perform it in me. Let me always be mindful of that so that I don't try to move ahead of You.

MY REFLECTION:

_____

_____

_____

_____

_____

_____

_____

_____

_____

DAY 5
JUSTIFIED

ROMANS 5:1

"Therefore being justified by faith, we have peace
with God through our Lord Jesus Christ."

*"Accordingly, now then being rendered just, innocent, and righteous by the
means of and because of our moral conviction of truth and the truthfulness
of God, our reliance upon and belief in God for our salvation, we are able
to possess, keep, and hold our peace, prosperity, rest, and being set at one
again together with and to be near the Supreme Divinity, God, by reason of
our Supreme in authority, Lord Jesus Christ, the anointed Messiah." (NWI)*

Those who have asked Jesus to come into their hearts and lives, and to be their Lord and Savior, have the ability to have peace and to hold onto it. The key is to not think about or dwell on the problem and concerns of life, but to rely on Him totally and completely. The Bible says we can actually "own" peace—it's ours, we possess it. But if we continue to fret, worry, be anxious, or be in fear instead of trusting the Lord for our circumstances, we are actually giving our peace away. God wants us to not only have and own peace but also to keep it and hold onto it.

This reminds me of a little girl who was given a beautiful necklace that had been her great-great-great grandmother's. It was a family treasure that had been passed down from mother to daughter for generations. Not fully understanding the importance or value of the necklace, the young girl carelessly laid it down somewhere and forgot it was there. The next day, she placed her drink on the same table, causing the valuable necklace to fall to the floor, under the table, back by the wall where it couldn't be seen. The next day, her Mom wanted her to wear the beautiful heirloom to church, but when the young girl went to look for it, she couldn't find it. Anxiety, fear, worry, and guilt entered her heart because she didn't know what she had done with it.

The same is true with our peace. If we don't treasure and value peace, rest, and all that God has provided for us, but carelessly "lay it down," we may lose it. We must hold onto, keep, and know the value of what God has given us so that we don't lose His precious gift of peace. We need to recognize its value, because when we carelessly toss it away, we instead carry guilt, worry, anxiety, and fear.

Lord, I pray that my eyes would be fixed on You instead of the problems I am facing, so that I can possess the peace You have graciously provided through Jesus Christ. Help me to understand its value so that I can hold onto Your peace and keep it when I am going through the difficulties of life.

MY REFLECTION:

_____

_____

_____

_____

_____

_____

_____

_____

_____

_____

_____

_____

_____

_____

_____

_____

_____

_____

_____

_____

_____

DAY 6
SANCTUARY

ISAIAH 8:13-14a

"Sanctify the Lord of hosts himself; and let him be your fear, and let him be your dread. And he shall be for a sanctuary."

"You need to keep holy, sanctify, and hallow the self-existent Jehovah, Lord of His army, organized for war, and let Him be your fear, dread, and what you reverence. And He will be for an asylum, a consecrated, and holy place." (NWI)

Instead of being afraid of the circumstances around us, we should have respect and fear for the One Who can take care of, answer, or deliver us from our problems—whatever they may be. Jehovah God is the "commander in chief" of His army, that is ready for battle on our behalf as we trust Him and keep Him in respect and awe. He has a full army of angels at His disposal to discharge on our behalf if needed. Our confidence should be in that truth, and not in what we can see, feel, or hear in the natural realm.

We need to recognize Who actually has the power and authority over the situation. The difficulties of life can be overwhelming, distracting, and frustrating, causing anger and fear, but our God is bigger than our situations and is more than able to do what is necessary to bring victory. When we put our hope, trust, and confidence in Him, we are surrendering those fears and problems to Him and allowing Him to do what needs to be done in His timing. When we do, we will be able to experience His peace that enables us to believe and continue rather than quit and give up.

One of the things that brings the most encouragement and hope to me in this verse is that the God that I put my hope and confidence in is literally in charge of His army of angels—angels that are ready at a moment's notice to do what's needed on my behalf. His army of angels are ready to war on my behalf when God gives the charge. So it doesn't matter what's coming against me. If I will just realize how holy He is, honor Him, and show Him praise, He will do whatever is needed for any situation I might face.

As I remember stories of God's exploits in His Word, my faith is built and I can believe for my victory. Remember how God delivered millions of His children from Pharaoh? How He turned water into wine at a wedding? How He closed the lion's mouths to keep them from eating Daniel? When he saved Noah and his family from an impending flood? Provided food for a widow? How He used Joshua to lead the Israelites to march around Jericho seven times and how the wall fell down when they shouted? There are so many miracles throughout God's Word that describe how the Lord moved on behalf of His people when they sought and honored Him. They build my faith to believe for my own circumstances.

Father, help me to stay focused on the fact that You are able! You are ready to do warfare on my behalf if needed. Therefore, no matter what I may be dealing with right now, you are bigger and able to do exceedingly, abundantly above what I could ask or think. You can do what is needed in my situation, and I trust You to take care of me and my loved ones.

MY REFLECTION:

DAY 7
WALK HONESTLY

ROMANS 13:13

"Let us walk honestly, as in the day; not in rioting and drunkenness, not in chambering and wantonness, not in strife and envying."

"Let us walk about decently, honorably, and honestly as in the daytime; not in carousing and reveling as if letting loose and being intoxicated and drunk, not in cohabitation and filthy vices, not in quarrels, debates, strife, heated jealousy, and envy." (NWI)

Are we so caught up in the ways and lifestyles of the world around us that we're not living the godly life He has provided for us? In this passage, Paul is instructing us to live honorably, honestly, and decently. What does that look like?

It means we should live our lives as if we can be seen by others because, in fact, there is always someone watching us. Are we reflecting Jesus or are we quarreling, causing strife, being envious of others, being drunk, having sex outside of marriage, and so on? Non-Christians watch us to see if what we have as Christians is better than what they have. They want to know if, when we have problems, we will handle them differently or fall apart like everyone else. They want to know if living for Jesus has any benefits. If we are trusting the Lord for our individual circumstances, we will be able to have peace, joy, hope, love, and forgiveness in the midst of the turmoil we are going through.

It's not that we won't hurt, grieve, have financial problems, or deal with other issues; but Jesus gives us peace in the middle of the storm, hope that He has it all under control, forgiveness and love for the person that betrayed us, and the ability to keep moving forward in life when the world would react differently because they don't have the Lord to help them through it all. What are we displaying for others to see?

I will never forget an incident that happened many years ago. A friend's son was sick and having trouble with his ears. I asked her if I could pray for him. Her response was something I didn't expect, but it has stuck with me and influenced me many times over the years. She said to me, "I've been watching you for three years, and because of that, I'll let you pray for my son." Wow! I understood at that moment that, whether I realized it or not, people are watching me all the time. Of course, initially, all I could think about were the times I'd yelled at my kids. . . . but thank God, she saw more. She saw the times I'd had various problems, and how I'd dealt with them. She saw that my relationship with the Lord was real and not something I only did on Sunday morning—she'd seen me live it out every day and in every circumstance. Trust me, I'm not saying that I always have my life perfectly all together, that I'm never afraid, that I never worry, or that I don't have troubles. Of course I do, and I struggle just like everyone else. But she saw that, in and through the difficulties of life, I lean on the Lord for my help.

What are others seeing in your day-to-day life? Are they seeing you live the same way on Monday through Saturday that you do Sunday morning? Are they seeing that, when you have problems, you seek the Lord for answers, or are they seeing you completely stressed out, worrying, and in fear? We need to live our lives as if someone is watching—because someone usually is.

> Father, help me to live in Your power, strength, and
> peace, that others may see Jesus living in me.

MY REFLECTION:

DAY 8
GLORIFY THE LORD

ISAIAH 24:15

"Wherefore glorify ye the LORD in the fires, even the name
of the LORD God of Israel in the isles of the sea."

*"In like manner, you should abound with honor and glorify the
Eternal Jehovah in the fire and light, even the individuality, honor,
authority, and character of the self- existent and eternal, Supreme
God of Jacob in the desirable islands of the seas." (NWI)*

When we are going through difficult times, it seems like everything is dark—it seems as if we are in the worst places. Nothing about our situation seems good or right. Everything is falling apart, hope is lost, we feel bad, and our troubles seem to be enclosing around us to the point that there doesn't appear to be any place that remotely seems "right." We can easily get "caught up" in the "woe is me" attitude and feel like nothing will ever be good or normal again. But this passage says even in the midst of the "fires," we should praise the Lord.

We can thank Him for His light, hope, and encouragement. We should glorify God for Who He is. Thank Him for the fact that He is your Healer, Wisdom, Strength, Comforter, Friend, Husband, Provider, Peace, Deliverer, Light in the darkness, and Way-Maker. We can give Him praise because He is everything we need. When we do, our empty feelings, concerns, and hopelessness will seem like a desirable, habitable "ocean-front" island resort surrounded by calming waves, provision, and blessing.

There is something so special about going to the beach for vacation—especially if it is a quiet, private island: the salty ocean air, gentle breezes, seagulls calling out, palm trees swaying, waves lapping on the sand, dolphins swimming by, sand crabs scurrying into their holes, burying your toes into the sand, and searching for the perfect shell. It calms your nerves, stills your fears. You get lost in the moments, and God can speak to you. That is what happens when we glorify the Lord during our times of difficulties. He is able to "put out the fires," "still the storms," give light in our darkness, and bring peace to our souls.

Lord, thank You for all that You have provided for me. Thank You for Who You are. When the difficulties of life come at me, help me to recognize Your goodness towards me. Help me to honor and praise You, that I may rest in Your provision and answers.

MY REFLECTION:

_____

_____

_____

_____

_____

_____

_____

_____

_____

_____

_____

_____

_____

_____

_____

_____

_____

_____

_____

_____

_____

_____

DAY 9
SALVATION

MARK 10:26-27

"And they were astonished out of measure, saying among themselves,
Who then can be saved? And Jesus looking upon them saith, With men
it is impossible, but not with God: for with God all things are possible."

This is one of my favorite verses because Jesus boldly, matter-of-factly, and with complete confidence declares that nothing is too difficult for God. There is no one that is "too far gone," no one that has too many riches or that has wandered too far away in his or her own lusts, no one that has committed too many sins, no one that says they don't even believe in God anymore, NO ONE that can't be saved. It is always still possible—that's why we must continue to pray for our family, friends, neighbors, community, state, country, leaders, and the world. Hearts can still be changed, and there is nothing impossible with God.

His desire is for "all men to be saved, and to come unto the knowledge of the truth" (1 Timothy 2:4). Jesus came to show us the truth in John 3:16: "For God so loved the world that he gave his only begotten Son, that whosoever believes in him should not perish, but have eternal life." Likewise, 1 Timothy 2:25 says, "For there is one God, and one mediator between God and men, the man Christ Jesus, Who gave himself a ransom for all."

Through these verses we see that God provided a way through His Son, Jesus Christ, for EVERYONE to be saved. It is His desire that we all ask Jesus to be our Lord and Savior, and that no one perishes. We also can see that God is able to do the impossible in order to bring us to a saving knowledge of Jesus. Therefore, let us come boldly before the throne of grace and pray for those we love, those who are lost, those who are bound with addictions, as well as those in authority over us, that they would ask Jesus to be their Lord and live for and with Him. Let's not quit interceding on their behalf so we can see what God will do!

Father, forgive me for not continuing to pray for the lost and believing for their salvation. I ask You to remind me to specifically pray for them. I believe Your Word is true, therefore, I believe for their salvation in Jesus's name.

MY REFLECTION:

_____
_____
_____
_____
_____
_____
_____
_____
_____
_____
_____
_____
_____
_____
_____
_____
_____
_____
_____
_____
_____
_____
_____

DAY 10
THE LORD HEARS

PSALM 34:17

"The righteous cry, and the Lord heareth, and
delivered them out of all their troubles."

*"When anyone cries out and gathers together with the Lord, the
self-Existent, Eternal God attentively hears, gives ear, and listens, and
defends, delivers, recovers, rescues, saves, and plucks them out of
adversity, affliction, anguish, distress, tribulation, or trouble." (NWI)*

When we decide to draw close to God in the midst of our problems and call out to Him, He not only hears us but also attentively listens to us. Not only does He listen to our problems, but He also does something about them. It is sometimes hard for me to grasp the fact that the God Who created the universe and everything in it actually hears and pays attention to me when I pray to Him or cry out to Him. But God's Word clearly shows us that's exactly what He does.

Repeatedly throughout scripture, God hears the cries of His people and answers their prayers. It may have taken longer than they wanted at times, but He answered them at just the right time.

How frustrating it is to try to tell someone about things we're dealing with—pouring out our heart to them—and to not have that person pay attention to us. Maybe they're doodling on paper or checking their texts and social media. You feel completely unheard, like it was a waste of your time to explain what's going on in your life. Then, another person may actually listen to what you have shared, say, "I'm sorry", and go about their business—not doing anything to help you. At least they took the time to listen, but it really wasn't of much benefit. Neither of these examples reflects how our God works! Not only does He attentively listen, but He also does something about our situations. It may not seem like He is acting as quickly as we want Him to at times, but this scripture clearly promises God will "rescue, save, deliver, recover" us from our troubles— whatever they might be.

Father, thank You for hearing my cries. Thank You for delivering, defending, recovering, rescuing, and saving me from adversity, affliction, anguish, distress, tribulation, and trouble of any kind. Thank You Lord that not only do You hear and listen to me, but that You also do what is needed to help me.

MY REFLECTION:

_____

_____

_____

_____

_____

_____

_____

_____

_____

_____

_____

_____

_____

_____

_____

_____

_____

_____

_____

_____

_____

_____

_____

DAY 11

CLOTHED IN RIGHTEOUSNESS

ROMANS 13:14
"But put ye on the Lord Jesus Christ, and make not provision for the flesh, to fulfil the lusts thereof."

"But invest with clothing yourself with the Supreme in authority, the Lord Jesus Christ, and don't take forethought or bring forth provision for the body, your human nature with its physical and moral passions, to long after, desire, and lust after forbidden things." (NWI)

I love this wording, "clothing yourself," because it helps me to more clearly understand what God's Word is telling me. When I put on my clothes, they cover the body parts I don't want others to see. In other words, in this passage, I would be covering the parts of me that have doubt, fear, anxiety, worry, discouragement, anger, lust, envy, and depression with Jesus's supreme power, strength, peace, hope, comfort, confidence, faith, and all that He has provided for me.

I decide whether I will put on my clothes in the natural, and I also decide moment by moment whether I will "put on" the clothing Jesus offers me that will help me to make it through life's issues. It almost reminds me of the "superheroes" in movies. They may be normal people working a job like everyone else one minute, but when there is a problem, they "put on" their superhero clothing and become someone else that can fight the battle ahead. With Jesus, we can become "superheroes," in essence, because when we have put on the clothes of His righteousness, He gives us all that we need to "get the job done" and be victorious.

Lord, help me to remember that, no matter the problems I may face, if I will just turn to You, You will "clothe me" with everything I need to be an overcomer. You may not take the problem away, but as I trust You, You will help me, equip me, and give me the peace to get through it all.

MY REFLECTION:

DAY 12

WHO IS ON THE LORD'S SIDE?

EXODUS 32:1

"And when the people saw that Moses delayed coming down out of the mount, the people gathered themselves together unto Aaron, and said unto him, Up, make us gods, which shall go before us: for as for this Moses, that man that brought us up out of the land of Egypt, we wot not what is become of him."

Moses had been up on the mountain getting God's ten commandments. It was a glorious time between Moses and the Lord, whereby the Lord was speaking to Moses and instructing him. But the children of Israel weren't privy to this one-on-one experience, so all they knew was that Moses had gone up to the mountain and hadn't come back. Because of that, they were once again murmuring and complaining—this time to Aaron, Moses' brother. The people told him to make gods for them to worship. Aaron instructed them to take off their earrings and bring them to him. He then received what they'd brought him and, after melting the gold, fashioned it into a molten calf.

The people said, "These be thy gods, O Israel, which brought thee up out of the land of Egypt" (verse 4). Aaron then built an altar before the calf and told them to worship the Lord there the next day, whereby they sat down to eat and drink and then rose up to play.

The Lord heard all of the commotion and knew what had occurred, so He told Moses to get down from the mountain because the people had corrupted themselves and had turned aside quickly from His commands. He told Moses that they'd made a molten calf and worshipped it, sacrificing themselves to it. God was *mad*—He was about to take out His wrath upon the people; but Moses interceded for them, reminding God that, if He slew them, the Egyptians would just say that God brought them out to kill them and not save them.

Moses also reminded God of His promise to Abraham, Isaac, and Jacob. God repented of what He wanted to do because of Moses' intercessory prayer for them. Moses went down the mountain with the two tables of stone carved and engraved by God Himself, but as soon as he heard and saw what was going on, he became angry and threw the tables out of his hands and broke them. Moses took the calf and burned it, ground it to powder and, after putting it in water, made the people drink it. Then, he asked them, "Who is on the LORD's side? Let him come unto me" (verse 26). The Lord told Moses to go back up the mountain and He would once again give him the Ten Commandments—but this time, Moses was going to have to carve the stone. The people could see the cloudy pillar (God's sign that He was present). When Moses came down and began giving the children of Israel God's commandments, he actually had to put a veil over his face because it shined so brightly from being in God's presence.

I wonder how many times we have been like the children of Israel. They were obedient as long as God was directly before them in a pillar of a cloud or fire, but when they had to wait on Him, they started doing what they thought was a good idea. God has done so many mighty miracles for us, and yet when we have to go for a period of time without His presence or voice to lead us, we get anxious and try to "get the job done" ourselves, just like they did. Instead of waiting patiently on the Lord with the last thing He instructed us to do, we get impatient and start thinking of ways to get the thing accomplished.

What does this look like today? After all, I doubt any of us are going to take our jewelry and melt it down to make a golden image to worship! But honestly, we are still doing the same basic thing that they did. For instance, God miraculously gives you a job, and at first you are so excited because you saw God work on your behalf, but it ended up not being what you thought it was going to be. You are not happy, and you're ready to leave to find something you would rather do. You start looking for another job—one that is more to your liking with different people that aren't going to bother you so much, or with a boss that appreciates you, or with the hours you would rather work, or with more money.

Instead of staying still and letting God use you where you are—or teach you what He needs you to know—you take it upon yourself to get out of there. Or maybe, you prayed for a spouse and God blessed you with someone. At first, everything is amazing, but as time wears on, he or she isn't quite the "angel" you thought they were going to be. You're upset that they snore, you resent that they don't clean up after themselves, and you are ready to get out of that relationship. There wasn't any physical abuse, and God didn't tell you to leave, you just want out and choose to have an affair or get a divorce.

There are endless scenarios that can occur along these lines, but the bottom line is that, instead of waiting on God's direction and leading, we take things into our own hands and "do something." It seems that we, like the Israelites, are willing to listen to God when He is right in front of us, leading us, but when we don't see or hear from Him for a while, we tend to forget and start doing our own thing. What He wants from us is to obey His last instructions and then wait on Him to give us the next set of directions. We may have no idea what God has in store for us right around the corner if we'll just wait patiently on Him!

Father, help me to wait on You, be still, and not try to figure things out in my own understanding. Help me to be obedient to what You told me to do without jumping to do my own will.

MY REFLECTION:

DAY 13
PROSPERING SOUL

3 JOHN 2

"Beloved, I wish above all things that thou mayest prosper
and be in health, even as thy soul prospereth."

*"Dearly beloved, I pray to God concerning everything pertaining
to you and your household, that they will succeed in reaching
prosperity and likewise be of sound health in your body and be safe,
just as your spirit, heart, life, mind, and soul prospers." (NWI)*

John has a sincere heart towards Gaius, who pastored a couple of churches but found himself having to deal with some issues. John is trying to encourage Gaius, which is something we all need from time to time. He let Gaius know that he was first of all praying for him. I have had people pray for me, and I can relate to the comfort it brings when someone lets you know they are lifting you up in prayer. In this case, John was a pillar in the faith, one of the original apostles who lived, learned, and walked with Jesus. So to be encouraged by someone like that is even more special.

John initiates the letter by telling Gaius that he is well-loved and prayed for. Then, he says that he is specifically praying that Gaius would prosper, as well as his whole household (family). One step further, John tells him that he also prays for health in his body and that he would be safe. We all want that, don't we? But here comes the contingency clause: "just like your spirit, heart, life, mind, and soul prospers." In other words, John is recognizing that Gaius is putting his all into serving the Lord, worshipping the Lord, and spending time with the Lord.

This begs the question: are we so sincere in our walk with the Lord that others would be able to pray blessings over us based on our prosperous walk with Him? Let me rephrase it this way: would I want someone to pray over me based on the amount of time and energy I place on my relationship with the Lord? Because if I am spending time in prayer, reading God's Word, and worshipping Him, my soul, spirit, and mind will reflect a life that isn't easily offended, will exhibit unconditional love, will serve others, will pray for other's needs, will forgive, and will live righteously. Living this kind of Christian life not only reflects Jesus to others but also enables us to be open and ready to receive God's prosperity in all areas of life.

> Father, I pray that my heart, mind, spirit and soul would be like Gaius'—that they would prosper.

MY REFLECTION:

_____

_____

_____

_____

_____

_____

_____

_____

_____

_____

_____

_____

_____

_____

_____

_____

_____

_____

_____

_____

_____

_____

DAY 14
SONLIGHT

JOHN 8:12

"Then spake Jesus unto them, saying, I am the light of the world: he that followeth me shall not walk in darkness, but shall have the light of life."

I am very blessed to live on a lake, where I love to look out our sunroom windows at the glistening waters. In the early hours of the morning, before my husband gets up, it is where I usually have my time with the Lord, reading my Bible and praying. One particular morning, as I was looking out the window during my quiet time, I noticed that my normal view of a breathtaking sunrise was presently a very rainy, dark, foggy, and cloudy scene. Houses, trees, landscapes, the lake—even the lights—were muffled, hard to distinguish, and even a little depressing. Things were definitely unclear.

This reminded me of seasons of our lives in which, yes, the sun has risen, but because of the weather we can't enjoy all that we would normally experience. Spiritually speaking, there are times when we know Jesus is in our midst, but because of all that is going on, it's hard to see Him clearly. Just as by simple faith I knew that the sun had risen that morning—even though everything was dark and clouded by the rain and fog and I couldn't actually see the sunrise—I must trust in the midst of difficult times, when it's hard to tell that Jesus is there, that He is. He is there! His light is still shining.

God is there with us, providing the little bit of light that we do have to be able to see through all of the storms of life. I had the realization that morning that the sun rose whether it was clearly visible or not. It still "rose" to give light in the darkness. It's an easy thing to recognize that the sun has risen—you can see the horizon get brighter and brighter when there are no clouds in the sky. But we need to remember that God is still there in our dark circumstances to give us light and visibility—to enable us to have hope, faith, and an awareness of His presence. No matter how dark it may appear to be, He has still "risen" to give us light in our darkness.

Lord, help me to remember that, whether I see You clearly through the circumstances I'm facing or not, You are still there. You haven't left me. I can trust that You are still with me. I may not see You as clearly as other times, but I can be assured that You are there!

MY REFLECTION:

DAY 15
WAITING

EXODUS 39:32

"Thus was all the work of the tabernacle of the tent of the
congregation finished: and the children of Israel did according
to all the LORD commanded Moses, so did they."

God had given Moses instructions on building the tabernacle, and Moses had then given those instructions to the children of Israel. They did everything just as they were instructed. I can only imagine the beauty of the attire for the priests and the majesty of the building itself. God directed each and every need, each and every step, each and every intricate detail. He put it on the hearts of individual people to do their jobs and make provision for the tabernacle, and they were totally obedient in their jobs.

How different this scenario is compared to the people waiting for Moses to come down off of the mountain! It's the "waiting" on the Lord that gets us in trouble, isn't it? We try to do our own thing and even seek out and follow others instead of doing what God has us doing: waiting for Him to bring us His Word. We are usually obedient to do things when He's given specific instructions, but when we have to wait—especially if it's longer than we think it should be, and we don't see any progress—we give up and do what we think is best in our own strength, ability, and understanding.

Many times, God puts us in a "holding pattern" in which we have to wait in quietness for His voice and His direction. This is for a reason. He may be trying to teach us something through the experience. He may want us to stay in that place to help someone. He may have people that can be helpful to us in that place. There are many reasons God places us in holding patterns, but we may not always know what they are. Just like when we fly in a plane, we have to trust the pilot when he circles around for a while or even reroutes the flight—we trust that he knows something we don't. In the same way, we must trust the Lord and do what He last instructed us to do instead of "going ahead" and doing our own thing. Usually, when we do our own thing, we get off course and in trouble, not realizing the Lord's delay was due to the fact that He knew something we didn't—a danger or problem of some kind.

Lord, help me to be obedient and to keep from doing things when You've not led me to do them. Help me to trust that You have my best interest in mind at all times and that You know what I need more than I do.

MY REFLECTION:

_____

_____

_____

_____

_____

_____

_____

_____

_____

_____

_____

_____

_____

_____

_____

_____

_____

_____

_____

_____

_____

_____

_____

DAY 16
LIGHT OR SHADOW?

LUKE 11:35

"Take heed therefore that the light which is in thee be not darkness."

"Take aim at, regard, consider, look at, and mark like a sentry, scout, or spy, accordingly that the rays that shine and make manifest to give light which is in you isn't obscured like a shadow." (NWI)

We need to be intentionally looking out, checking ourselves, and watching to be sure that the light of Jesus which is in us doesn't grow dim and merely reveal shadows of Him rather than exposing what is real.

We need to allow the light of Jesus to shine from us for all to see Him. We need to be sure that others are seeing the fullness of His light in us. If we aren't doing that, we cannot be quite as effective as witnesses, because others are only seeing "a shadow" of Jesus and not the real thing. If we are living in the fullness of His light, it will draw others to Him. When we are only revealing a shadow of Him, others don't understand exactly what they are seeing in us, and it isn't much different than the darkness they are in already. In order to draw people to Jesus, we need to do what Jesus told us in Matthew 5:14-16: "Ye are the light of the world. A city that is set on an hill cannot be hid. Neither do men light a candle, and put it under a bushel, but on a candlestick; and it gives light to all that are in the house. Let your light so shine before men, that they may see your good works, and glorify your Father which is in heaven."

When we have Jesus living inside of us, He will shine through us so that others will be drawn to His light.

Father, help me to allow the light of Jesus that is within me to shine brighter each day as I walk closer to You. I pray that You will be glorified and draw others to Yourself through my life.

MY REFLECTION:

_____

_____

_____

_____

_____

_____

_____

_____

_____

_____

_____

_____

_____

_____

_____

_____

_____

_____

_____

_____

_____

DAY 17
THE IMPOSSIBLE

PSALM 66:5-6

"Come and see the works of God: he is terrible in his doing toward the children of men. He turned the sea into dry land: they went through the flood on foot: there did we rejoice in him."

Most of us are probably familiar with the account of what God did for the Israelites when the Egyptians were chasing them and they encountered the Red Sea. A friend of mine once wrote, "Where's the boat?" I imagine the Israelites wondered that very question when they came to the Red Sea with no way to cross it, the Egyptians racing in chariots toward them. That would have been *my* first thought, right after, "How can we get across here?" I certainly wouldn't have been able to swim fast enough—if I could do it at all! The thoughts that must have been running rampant in their minds—the great concerns, and the notion that God had brought them out of Egypt only to be killed in the Red Sea—probably ravaged them with gripping fear. But God didn't provide boats, the only rational way of crossing, especially in a hurry. He did the *impossible*!

This made me wonder . . .

I wonder how many times I have put God in a box because of my own understanding. How many times have I limited God because I could only see one or two possible ways of getting something done, when He had a much better way I couldn't even imagine? Because of our limitations, we tend to get frustrated, we quit, we grow weary, we lose hope, and we get scared. Our trust is in what we see and can understand instead of in what God can do.

God sees the bigger picture. He is all-powerful. He has all understanding. He can do exceedingly, abundantly above what we can ask or even think. The Israelites couldn't even think—let alone comprehend—God doing something as big as causing the waters to stand up so they could walk on newly-dry ground. That's too big. *Nevertheless, God did it!*

So, what's impossible in your life? I have a list of things in my life. Let's get our eyes on the One Who can part the sea rather than keeping them on the "deep waters" in front of us. Let's not try to figure out how God can bring us a "big enough boat," but instead trust Him to do what only He can do. He is the God of impossibilities that delights to show us the "more than we could ask or think." Even when things seem to be doom and gloom, He has a bigger plan that we may not be able to see yet that will safely and gloriously bring us to the other side. Glory to God!

Lord, help me to think about the fact that You are able to do the impossible rather than keeping my eyes on the impossible thing in front of me. Help me to see the bigger picture You have for me. Help me to realize You have a purpose and plan for my life. Help me to understand that, even though I can only see the limitations, You are able to see everything. Lord, I trust You.

MY REFLECTION:

_____

_____

_____

_____

_____

_____

_____

_____

_____

_____

_____

_____

_____

_____

_____

_____

_____

_____

_____

_____

DAY 18
ASSEMBLING

HEBREWS 10:25
"Not forsaking the assembling of ourselves together, as
the manner of some is; but exhorting one another: and so
much the more, as ye see the day approaching."

Many people choose to stay home from church. There are many reasons for this, such as having an illness, a fear of contracting some disease (like COVID or the flu), the convenience of watching church online, or having been hurt by someone—the list goes on. Whatever the reason, Hebrews 10:25 encourages us to assemble together.

When we meet in person to have church, we are encouraged, strengthened, and our faith is built up. What a difference it makes to know you are not alone with your problems! Of course, you can be spiritually fed watching services online, or evangelists on TV, but there is something special about being there in person. It's like the difference between watching a game on TV and being there in person, or going to a concert versus listening to a song on the radio. You can certainly be blessed and enjoy watching the game on TV or listening to a song on the radio, but how much better is it when you can experience it all live and in person!

Plus, it's just a lot more fun being with other Christians and friends. We need each other! If you are attending a church in person, you know this to be true. There is a lot of work to be done for the kingdom of God and we can definitely get more accomplished when we work together. As much as we see going on around us every day, we definitely need to join hand-in-hand with Christian brothers and sisters to stand, encourage, love, pray for, and show compassion for one another as we endure these latter days.

Father, I pray for those who cannot attend church for whatever reason—I
pray that people would be healed, provision made, and hearts mended.
I pray that those who are able to attend church would start getting
involved with their local church. I pray for anyone who doesn't have

a church home, that they would be able to find one in which to get involved. I pray that we would join hands to further the kingdom of God and be the hands and feet of Jesus to minister to those in need.

MY REFLECTION:

_____

_____

_____

_____

_____

_____

_____

_____

_____

_____

_____

_____

_____

_____

_____

_____

_____

_____

_____

_____

DAY 19
CHOSEN

ISAIAH 41:8
"But thou, Israel, art my servant, Jacob whom I have chosen, the seed of Abraham my friend."

God called Israel His servant, but He told Israel that he was chosen when he had been Jacob. The word *chosen* means, "select, acceptable, appoint, choose, (choice), excellent, join." In other words, even when Jacob was a supplanter—when he held his twin brother Esau's heel in his mother's womb trying to be the firstborn, and when he later cheated away his brother's birthright by lying and deceiving his father, Isaac—God still chose him and counted him to be "accepted and excellent."

Jacob knew the importance of being the eldest son and receiving the blessing of his father—unlike Esau, who apparently didn't appreciate what it entailed. Jacob even wrestled with an angel and won, whereby his name was changed to Israel. How can this be? Didn't God see all that Jacob had done? Yes, He did! But because Jacob was Abraham's seed (his grandson), and because He saw in Jacob more than even Jacob knew about Himself, God chose him.

God has chosen each of us, despite what we have done in our past. He sees things in us that we don't see or understand. If we accept Jesus as our Lord and Savior, He calls us His sons and daughters and we are accepted as His own. Just like Jacob was accepted and chosen despite his past, we are as well.

If you have never asked Jesus to be your Lord and Savior, I would encourage you to do so now. It's simple to do. All you have to do is ask Him into your heart and to forgive you of your sins. As Isaiah 43:5a says: "Fear not: for I am with you . . . " You have nothing to fear. Don't get me wrong—He's not some "Sugar Daddy." But He will be your Father, Healer, Comforter, Savior, Provider, Deliverer, Defender, Joy, Help, and Peace. Just like Jacob became God's servant, we have been "bought" by the death and resurrection of Jesus, to be set free of our past and present sins and become His sons and daughters. Jacob was who he was—a liar and deceiver—but Israel is how God saw him: the seed of Abraham. As a child of God, we can be our best selves. Even if you have already asked Jesus into your heart, it is a good thing to daily surrender to His Lordship.

Father, I come to You today, surrendering my life to You. I give You all that I am and ask You to help me become who You have for me to be. I ask Jesus to be the Lord of my life today and every day.

MY REFLECTION:

_____

_____

_____

_____

_____

_____

_____

_____

_____

_____

_____

_____

_____

_____

_____

_____

_____

_____

_____

_____

_____

_____

DAY 20
POWER, LOVE, AND A SOUND MIND

2 TIMOTHY 1:7

"For God has not given us a spirit of fear; but of power,
and of love, and of a sound mind." (NKJV)

*"Seeing then that God, the Supreme Divinity has not given us a
spirit of fear or timidity; but of miraculous power, ability, strength,
dear love, and of a self-controlled sound mind." (NWI)*

I don't think we truly understand what God has done for us—or maybe I should say, *I* don't. If we did, we would be walking in the fullness of what God has provided for us through the life, death, and resurrection of Jesus Christ.

This passage clearly says we shouldn't have any doubts about who we are. Paul was writing this letter to Timothy, whom he described as someone with sincere love without hypocrisy, like his grandmother, Lois, and his mother, Eunice. In other words, Timothy came from a family of believers. But in verse 6, Paul is reminding Timothy to stir up the gift of God that is in him. In verses 8 and 9, Paul continues to encourage Timothy not to be ashamed of his testimony of the Lord, who saved him and called him with a holy calling according to Christ's own purpose.

We should realize that our shy and timid stance for the Lord is incorrect. We tend to act like wimps with no strength, but these verses contradict that posture completely. Verse 7 declares boldly that we should be walking in God's miraculous power, His ability, His strength, His love, and His self-control that gives us a sound mind, knowing who we are in Christ. We need to remember that what we do for the Lord is not done in our own strength or ability, because we won't have enough. But it is God that gives us the power, love, and sound mind to do what He has called us to do.

We don't have to be in fear or be timid about sharing our faith or testimony. Instead, we can be bold in His miraculous power, ability, strength, dear love, self-control, and sound mind. Notice also that Timothy was already living a life of love towards others that wasn't deceitful and hypocritical. He just needed a little "nudge" by Paul to walk in the fullness of what God had for him.

This is a great reminder for us as well. Like Timothy, we need to remember all God has done for us and be willing to share it with others without being afraid of what they might think. We can't be so timid that others don't hear us. This passage is a reminder to walk in love and do everything in God's timing. When God gives us that prick in our spirit to say something with love, clarity, boldness, and in the power of the Holy Spirit—the very power that raised Jesus from the dead—we should obey. We shouldn't be unkind, hurtful, critical, or judgmental of what others are doing, which is why we need God's sincere love, but we do need to share what God has done in our lives to be a source of hope and encouragement to others going through similar circumstances. Others need to know that God brought you through your situation, and that He can do the same for them.

> Father, I pray You would use me to help people I come into contact with to know Your faithfulness. Help me to live out this verse. Help me to know who to share my testimony with, and when I do, show me how to clearly declare what You have done in my life so that those who I talk to will feel Your presence and have hope in their lives.

MY REFLECTION:

_____

_____

_____

_____

_____

_____

_____

_____

_____

_____

_____

_____

_____

DAY 21

ARE YOU A CHRISTIAN?

PROVERBS 3:5-6 (NKJV)
"Trust in the LORD with all your heart, and lean not unto
your own understanding. In all your ways acknowledge
Him and He shall direct your paths."

*"Trust, be bold, confident, and sure in the Eternal Jehovah Lord with
your heart, feelings, will, or intellect and don't support yourself or
lean on your own understanding, knowledge, or wisdom. In all your
conversations, life, manners, or actions know, recognize, and be aware of
Him and He will make your way straight and direct your path." (NWI)*

Years ago, I was in fear. One night when I was alone, someone tried—almost successfully—to break into our little apartment. Quite frankly, it shook me pretty badly.

We bought and moved to a new house in a different town, but from that moment on, for almost two years, I would constantly think I heard noises, or think someone was in our house. At times, I was paralyzed with fear. Finally, one night, the Lord very purposely asked me, "Nancy, are you a Christian?"

I replied, "Yes, Lord."

He responded, "Then act like one and trust me."

Wow! Talk about being a deer in headlights! It was one of those "aha" moments that has stuck with me ever since. Over the course of all of the years since, the Lord has repeatedly reminded me of that statement: "Nancy, are you a Christian? Then act like one and trust me." When I've faced uncertainties in life, I am reminded to trust the Lord. Admittedly, some of these times have been easier than others. But I can honestly say that, every single time, when I've decided to stop allowing fear to grip me and instead trust the Lord for the situation, He is always faithful to give me peace. What an amazing exchange—my fear for His peace!

So I am going to give you the same challenge God gave me. Are you a Christian? If so, then act like one and trust the Lord! Are you gripped with fear? Are you worried, stressed, anxious, uncertain, or angry? Do you not know how something can possibly turn out the way you need it to? Are you concerned about your family, your country, your children, health issues, or financial struggles? Then act like the Christian you declare yourself to be, and trust the Lord with your concerns. Allow Him to give you peace instead of the anguish you are feeling. I'm not going to pretend that every problem will go away or work out the way you want it to be resolved. But I can confidently assure you that, without fail, if you trust Him with the concern and stop trying to figure it all out, He will give you that peace that passes understanding to know that He will work it out for your good.

Continue to humbly bring your concerns before the Lord and leave them at His feet, and He will faithfully give you peace. Maybe He has a bigger plan than you can imagine. Maybe there is something He needs to do in you that you didn't even realize needed to be done. No matter what, God will give us the peace we so desperately need to carry us through the difficult times we are facing.

> Father, I come to You today in the name of Jesus, asking You to show me the ways I am not acting like the child of God You have called me to be. Show me how to trust You in every area of my life. When I am tempted to be in fear, remind me of who I am in You and that I can trust You to take care of me and whatever I am going through.

MY REFLECTION:

_____

_____

_____

_____

_____

_____

_____

_____

_____

_____

DAY 22
I WILL SAY

PSALM 91:2

"I will say of the Lord, He is my refuge and my
fortress; my God; in him will I trust."

*"I will report and tell about the Lord; He is my hope, my
place for refuge, protection, and shelter, my God; in Him
will I have confidence, security, and hope." (NWI)*

What is coming out of our mouths? We are not only told to think about God's Word, but according to this verse, we are to actually SAY the Word of God over ourselves and our situations, as well as declaring WHO God is in the situations.

We can see godly men and women in the Bible declaring their confessions of faith in dangerous or difficult situations. We are no different than they and need to declare what God's Word says, not what we feel about our circumstances. For example, Paul declares in 2 CORINTHIANS12:10, "Therefore I take pleasure in infirmities, in reproaches, in necessities, in persecutions, in distresses for Christ's sake: for when I am weak, then am I strong." Paul knew in and of Himself he was too weak to endure it all, but with Jesus, He was made strong enough to do what was necessary.

When we say aloud, "God, You are my refuge, my fortress, my Lord, my God, my healer, my deliverer, my Savior and I put my hope and trust in You", we become more and more confident in His protection, promises, provision, help, etc. Power and faith are released in us so that we believe God is able. We are speaking life over our situation. We may know what God's Word says about things, but until we speak His Word out loud, declaring Who God is, we haven't really put our faith to work.

Father, I declare You are my strength when I am weak,
You are my Healer when I am sick or infirmed, You are my
hope when I have no hope, You are my All in All.

MY REFLECTION:

DAY 23
OUR STRENGTH

ISAIAH 25:4

"For thou hast been a strength to the poor, a strength to the needy in his distress, a refuge from the storm, a shadow from the heat, when the blast of the terrible ones is as a storm against the wall."

"For you have been a stronghold, fortified place, and rock to the person who is weak, needy, or poor, a stronghold, fortified place, and rock to a person feeling destitute and needy in his affliction, anguish, distress, sorrow, and trouble, a shelter and place of hope and trust from the feeling of being carried away as with a flood; a defense and place of shade from heat and drought, when the anger and whirlwinds of the mighty oppressors are as if you are being carried away with a flood and feeling poured out and you are against a wall." (NWI)

Wow—I don't know if you've ever felt like you were being carried away by a flood, poured out with nothing else to give, or against a wall with no place to go. Maybe right now you're feeling destitute, full of anguish, needy, sorrowful, or distressed. I sure have. On differing occasions, I've felt all of those at once. But this verse declares that God is our stronghold. When we feel all of those things, He is our hope and trust. We may not have answers in or of ourselves, but if we give all of our problems, disappointments, and hurts, to the One who has the answers, He will bring peace to our storms.

I know God is faithful because He has brought me through more storms in life than I can count or even remember. He hears us when we cry out to Him, even though at times He may not answer as quickly as we would like. But I can 100% guarantee that if we seek Him, give Him our problems and fears, and allow Him to work in and for us, He will without fail fulfill His Word in our lives, and we will get the victory and the peace. He is faithful to fulfill His Word!

Father God, I turn all of my problems to You, knowing that You are my hope. I trust You, Lord, to bring me through. Forgive me for when I have doubted or tried to figure things out in my own ability rather than giving it all to You. Thank You, Lord, for taking care of me and helping me through the storms of life that seem to be powerful. I know that You are more powerful.

MY REFLECTION:

_____

_____

_____

_____

_____

_____

_____

_____

_____

_____

_____

_____

_____

_____

_____

_____

_____

_____

_____

_____

_____

_____

DAY 24
RELY ON JESUS

2 CORINTHIANS 1:24b

"... for by faith ye stand."

"... for by your assurance, belief, and reliance upon Christ for your salvation you abide, continue, hold up, and stand." (NWI)

When we are going through struggles of any kind—relational, emotional, financial, mental, or physical—the way we are able to continue on is by relying on Jesus. It's turning over our problems to Him and trusting Him with them. Trying to rely on your own strength, ability, wisdom, or understanding can only get you so far; at some point, you'll run out of resources and become stressed, depressed, angry, hopeless, or fearful.

I have come to realize over the years that, when I am feeling stressed, it's because I am trying to do everything myself. The Lord brought this to my attention when I was teaching school. I started off teaching in public school, stayed home for almost seven years to be a stay-at-home mom, taught at a Christian school for five years, stayed home for three years, and then went back to a public school. At first, I was nervous, having been away for so long. Basically everything I did was with much prayer. But over time, things became easier and I didn't rely on the Lord as much because I knew what I was doing.

Before long, I started getting really stressed about things—especially not being able to get everything done—and I noticed that problems were really getting to me. One day, I came to the realization that I had basically left the Lord out of my everyday life at school and was trying to do it all in my own strength and ability. I asked the Lord to forgive me and to lead and guide me through every situation that occurred at school, big or small. It may seem unnecessary to some, because I was "handling" everything, and "knew" what I was doing. The thing was, though, I honestly needed God's help, as evidenced by the fact that I was stressed all the time. I'm not saying that I never had another problem, because that would be a blatant lie; but what the Lord did was give me wisdom, discernment, peace, understanding, strength, and everything I needed to get the job done without going crazy in the middle of it all.

Now, when I start feeling stressed about something, I recognize it as the result of trying to do too much in my own ability and not turning it all over to the Lord. Yes, He had given me the gifts and talents needed to teach, but I can attest to the fact that things work much more smoothly when I include the Lord in the everyday things of my life.

Jesus will give you the "peace that passes understanding," which "will keep your hearts and minds" (Philippians 4:7). In other words, you will be and feel at peace even though your world may be crashing down around you. It's not that your circumstances necessarily change, but when you hand them to Jesus, He will exchange your stress for peace and confidence that it will all work out.

Lord, when I feel stress or fear, I know that it is a result of my trying to take care of a problem that is bigger than I can handle. I choose to give each problem or concern to You, because I know that You are able. I trust You, Lord!

MY REFLECTION:

DAY 25
BROKEN

JEREMIAH 4:3b

"Break up your fallow ground, and sow not among thorns."

"Break up and till the soil until it glistens, your freshly plowed land, and do not plant or conceive seed near, under, or among pricking thorns that spend the harvest season." (NWI)

This verse tells us to "break up your fallow ground." The words "break up" mean "the idea of the gleam of a fresh furrow; to till the soil" and "fallow" means "plowing freshly plowed land." This indicates that there should be a second tilling before planting. In other words, you till the ground, but then you do it again repeatedly until the soil glistens. I have to be honest—I've never seen the soil glisten, which may explain my lack of a good harvest!

Even though we may feel like the Lord has broken us, He still needs to make sure our "soil" is broken to the place that we glisten. Many people, including myself, have wondered why it feels like we've been broken over and over again, but this scripture is the answer. There is a reason we have to be broken more than once. For us to "shine" Jesus so that others desire Him, we must be broken and "tilled" until the "ground" of our hearts is ready to be planted with the good seed of His Word. If the soil isn't properly tilled, the seeds will be growing among the thorns of our past and won't produce as much fruit in our lives.

Further instructions in this verse indicate that we are not to throw out seeds among the thorns, because this will cause problems for the harvest. This is pretty understandable, but the wording here indicates we shouldn't even throw our seeds *near* thorns. This might explain why people have a difficult time when they've supposedly done all the right things, but they are still near the things that could cause them trouble. They are not living the fruitful life they could be living.

Once our "ground" is tilled and tilled until we are "glistening Jesus," we need to be sure to throw our seed on that tilled ground and not where the thorns and weeds once were. In other words, once we've been saved and delivered from things, it is important to not hang out with the same people we used to hang out with, who will bring us back into the same bad habits from which the Lord delivered us. As a matter of fact, we shouldn't even go near them. He has provided a way of escape, and we shouldn't go back to our old ways.

> Lord, help me to not murmur and complain when You are "refining me" and "breaking me." Help me to realize You are getting rid of the "thorns" in my life. I pray that, as You do this, I would be more and more like You so that others may look at me and see You.

MY REFLECTION:

_____

_____

_____

_____

_____

_____

_____

_____

_____

_____

_____

_____

_____

_____

_____

_____

_____

_____

_____

_____

DAY 26
NOT BY SIGHT

2 CORINTHIANS 5:7

"For we walk by faith, not by sight."

"For we walk at large because we are able, and we live by moral conviction of the truthfulness of God and our reliance, assurance, and belief in Christ, not by what we can see, have knowledge of, understand, or perceive." (NWI)

We should live our daily lives relying on God, being convicted by the truthfulness of God found in His Word, and believing in Jesus Christ. It is by our faith that we do this and not because of our knowledge, understanding, or experience. We don't see the truth of the gospel and then decide to believe. There are many instances and illustrations of this in the Bible, but a favorite involves Noah and his family.

The Bible says Noah was a righteous man who respected God. God told Noah to build a gigantic boat, which some say took him anywhere from 50-120 years to complete. That in and of itself is amazing, but up until this point, mankind had never seen a boat and didn't know what it was. In addition, until this moment, there had never been rain, so they didn't know what that was, either.

Let's go one step further. God told Noah to collect two of every animal except the clean animals for sacrifice, of which there would be seven each. These animals are normally enemies that kill each other—and they were all cooped up together for about a year. But Noah did everything out of faith, his reliance centered on God for their salvation. Even though everyone around him made fun of them during the ark's building, Noah and his family continued doing what God told him, regardless of whether it made any sense. Notice that his faith to do what God spoke to him came *before* their salvation from God's wrath on the earth. Just like 2 Corinthians 5:7 says, Noah and his family obeyed God's instructions by faith before they saw what was to happen.

Lord, help me to walk by faith like Noah and trust You for what I don't yet understand or even see. Help me to not be concerned with what others might think, but rather simply be obedient to what You have told me to do.

MY REFLECTION:

DAY 27
OVERWHELMED

JONAH 2:7

"When my soul fainted within me, I remembered the Lord, and
my prayer came in unto thee, into thine holy temple."

*"When my breathing, vitality, appetite, desire, heart, mind, and soul
languished, fainted, became feeble, and overwhelmed within me, I
remembered, became mindful, kept in remembrance, and thought
on the Eternal Lord, and my intercession and prayer came and abode
in unto You, into Your sacred, consecrated, holy temple." (NWI)*

There are times in our lives when it seems like everywhere we go, everyone we meet, and every piece of news we hear is bad. Whether it be issues in physical health, finances, marriage, children, jobs, aging parents, neighbors, or friends, this news can cause us to feel overwhelmed, faint, like we can't breathe. It can take away our appetite. But what Jonah did when he had those feelings was what we need to do: think on the Lord, keep Him and His Word in remembrance, and intercede and pray to Him.

Jonah was miserable because he was wallowing in self-pity. God told him to speak to the people of Nineveh to warn them of God's judgment if they didn't repent. Well, lo and behold, they took the message to heart and repented, changing God's heart to destroy them. Whether Jonah was mad or embarrassed, the bottom line is, he was upset at God. He'd finally obeyed the Lord and spoken His Word, but God hadn't "zapped" them. Jonah had personally judged the Ninevites and didn't like that God was giving them a second chance. It so upset Jonah that he could hardly think straight and was in deep depression and feeling faint. He wasn't turning it all over to the Lord. He wanted to be obedient, but thought he knew what God should do.

However, God saw the heart of the Ninevites, and because they repented, God changed His mind about bringing judgment on them. This gives us a prime example of how we can't prejudge people, because we don't really necessarily know their hearts. We also need to remember that we are not God. Only He knows the total situation and the hearts of those involved.

Even though it took Jonah a while to get past his anger issues, when he finally did turn to the Lord, the Lord heard his prayer and ministered to him. Whatever is going on in your life, whether from outside circumstances or self-imposed problems, turn it all over to the Lord, and He will bring you clarity and peace. He hears your prayers.

> Father, help me to have Your eyes, Your ears, and Your heart so that, as I obey Your voice, I will take my hands off the situation I am dealing with and realize You have it all under control.

MY REFLECTION:

_____

_____

_____

_____

_____

_____

_____

_____

_____

_____

_____

_____

_____

_____

_____

_____

_____

_____

DAY 28
HAVE MERCY

MATTHEW 17:15

"Lord, have mercy on my son: for he is a lunatick, and sore vexed:
for ofttimes he falleth into the fire, and oft into the water."

*"Supreme in authority, Lord God, have compassion and mercy on my son: for
he is crazy and a lunatic, he is moonstruck, and suffers badly and miserably
with a painful sensation: for he frequently has fallen down backward as a
result of the lightning, and many times as a result of the rain showers." (NWI)*

W as the son afraid of the lightning and rain, or had he been struck by lightning and electro-
cuted? There's no way of knowing, but whatever it was, the son was acting crazily, unable
to think or act normally to the point where his father asked Jesus to heal him. This could
actually have been a form of PTSD; whatever it was, it was a powerful, serious issue that had control
over the son. Each of us has things in our lives that have caused us to be in fear, lose control of our
actions and behaviors, or may even cause people to think we are "crazy."

Notice what the father does in this verse. He approaches Jesus by identifying Him as "supreme
in authority" and asking Him to have "compassion and mercy." The father showed his respect for
Jesus and identified Him as the One with the power and authority to help his son. He knew Jesus
was bigger than the problem.

Do we truly believe that Jesus is bigger than our problems? Jesus has all authority in heaven and
earth. We need to realize that, whatever we are facing—whatever brings fear to our heart, whatever
we are anxious about, whatever we are addicted to, or whatever tries to control us—must come
under the name of Jesus who is supreme in authority.

Jesus, have mercy and compassion on me. When I seem to be out of control
or not able to handle life, have mercy on me. I recognize that You are
supreme in authority over my problems. I acknowledge my areas of pain,

misery, and imperfection. As I declare You to be in authority over every area of my life, I know that You will set me free just like You did this son.

MY REFLECTION:

_____

_____

_____

_____

_____

_____

_____

_____

_____

_____

_____

_____

_____

_____

_____

_____

_____

_____

_____

_____

_____

_____

_____

DAY 29

DELIGHTING IN GOD'S WORD

PSALM 119:143

"Trouble and anguish have taken hold on me: yet
thy commandments are my delights."

*"Adversity, affliction, anguish, distress, sorrow, and
tribulation have occurred to me: Your commandments
and precepts are my delight and pleasure." (NWI)*

The psalmist is sharing his heart. He was struggling big time; but in and through it all, he realized that God's Word brought him pleasure and delight.

Even when we are in the midst of problems, we can have joy. We can have God's peace and joy when we are sad, hurt, sick, stressed, grieving, going through personal, physical, financial, family, work, or whatever our problems are. Our joy is not dependent on everything in our life being good or perfect. Psalm 16:11b says, "in thy presence is fullness of joy." When we are going through difficulties, the way we can find joy is to be in the presence of the Lord. Psalm 95:2 says, "Let us come before his presence with thanksgiving" and Psalm 100:2 says, "come before his presence with singing." By being both thankful for God's blessings in our lives as well singing His praises, we will become joyful. Reading God's Word brings joy as we reflect on His promises and blessings. It builds our faith and enables us to think beyond what we can see, hear or feel, It settles our spirit and brings peace, hope, encouragement, faith, and joy. Another way that God brings joy into our lives is by helping and serving others, whether at church, bringing food to sick neighbors and friends, or wherever there is a need.

Father, I pray that no matter what comes my way, I will put my trust in You, read Your Word, and praise You. I know You will give me Your peace and bring joy. Thank You, Lord, for Your Word.

MY REFLECTION:

_____

_____

_____

_____

_____

_____

_____

_____

_____

_____

_____

_____

_____

_____

_____

_____

_____

_____

_____

_____

_____

_____

_____

DAY 30
GOD'S FREEDOM

I CORINTHIANS 6:12

"All things are lawful unto me, but all things are not expedient: all things
are lawful for me, but I will not be brought under the power of any."

*"All, everyone, in every way, whatsoever and all manner of things
are right and allowed to be done in public, but all of it is not an
advantage, good, or makes us better for doing them: everything
is lawful for me, but I will not be brought under their control,
authority, or power, as if I were inferior to their power." (NWI)*

Just because we can do anything because of the freedom we have in Jesus Christ doesn't mean we should do everything we want to do. Many things will bring us to a place of bondage, such as addictive behaviors and substances. Some things will be detrimental to us emotionally, some will be harmful to us physically, some things will be embarrassing, and some things will cause the name of Jesus to be shamed.

Even though we have freedom, it's not in our best interest to do some things. For instance, I am free to put my hand into a burning fire, but it doesn't mean I won't get burned; I am free to drive 110 miles per hour on a road, but I run the risk of having a wreck and/or killing myself or someone else; I am free to buy everything I want, but it doesn't mean I won't have financial problems. I am free, but there are consequences to my behaviors. Some things will actually cause me not only to suffer their associative repercussions but also to be in bondage. In addition, many times, our behaviors will cause nonbelievers to turn away from the saving grace of Jesus Christ because they don't see that our lives are any different than theirs.

So I must ask myself whether what I'm doing is something good for me, something that draws others to Jesus, and something that allows me to live in freedom. Or, instead, is what I am doing (even though I am allowed to do it) going to be harmful for me and others? My ultimate purpose as a Christian is to live in the freedom of Jesus. That means we are not to live entangled in the snares of life. Freedom isn't freedom if what we choose to do is actually putting us in bondage to someone or something.

Lord, help me to live in Your freedom, which brings peace, contentment, and rest. If there is anything in my life drawing me or others away from You, reveal it to me, that I may repent and live in Your freedom, peace, and contentment. Help me to live a life that reflects Your freedom, so that others will see the difference and want to know You.

MY REFLECTION:

_____

_____

_____

_____

_____

_____

_____

_____

_____

_____

_____

_____

_____

_____

_____

_____

_____

_____

_____

DAY 31
PRAISE THE LORD

PSALM 148-150

"Praise ye the LORD. . . . from the heavens: praise him in the heights . . . all his angels . . . all his hosts . . . sun and moon . . . all ye stars of light . . . heavens of heavens . . . waters that be above the heavens . . . ye dragons . . . all deeps . . . fire, and hail: snow, and vapours: stormy wind fulfilling his word . . . mountains . . . all hills . . . fruitful trees . . . all cedars . . . beasts . . . all cattle; creeping things . . . flying fowl: kings of the earth . . . all people; princes, and all judges of the earth . . . young men, and maidens; old men, and children . . . Let them praise the name of the Lord: for his name alone is excellent; his glory is above the earth and heaven. . . . Praise ye the LORD. Sing unto the LORD a new song. . . . Let them praise his name in the dance. . . . with the timbrel and harp . . . Let the saints be joyful in glory. . . . sing aloud upon their beds. Let the high praises of God be in their mouth, and a two-edged sword in their hand. . . . Praise God in his sanctuary. . . . praise him for his mighty acts. . . . according to his excellent greatness . . . with the sound of the trumpet . . . with the psaltery and harp . . . the timbrel and dance . . . with stringed instruments and organs . . . upon the loud cymbals . . . upon the high sounding cymbals . . . *Let everything that has breath praise the* LORD. *Praise ye the* LORD."

Reading Psalm 148–150 reminds us of the psalmist's encouragement to praise the Lord. Sometimes, when life gets crazy, overwhelming, painful, confusing, stressful—fill in the blank—we forget to praise the Lord, the Creator of the universe. Whatever our reason for forgetting, it's not valid. I totally understand having a difficult time finding things to be thankful for when all you can see around you are the negative things. But that's the exact time and reason we should praise Him!

When we praise the Lord, it changes our focus from the negative to the positive, from the impossibility to the possibility, from discouragement to hope, from unbelief to faith. Somehow, praising God for what He has done, what He has provided, and what His Word says changes our outlook.

So, who does God's Word say should praise the Lord? Let's take a look: angels, His hosts, sun, moon, stars, heavens of heavens, waters above the heavens, dragons, all deeps, fire, hail, snow, vapor, stormy wind, mountains, hills, fruit trees, all cedars, beasts, all cattle, creeping things, flying fowl, kings of the earth, all people, princes, all judges of the earth, young men, maidens, old men, children, Israel, and everything that has breath. That covers everything and everyone, doesn't it?

For what should we praise Him? Praise Him for creating everything, His mighty acts, His excellent greatness, for the fact that His name alone is excellent, and for the truth that His glory is above the earth and heaven.

How should we praise Him? Sing praises to Him, rejoice in Him, praise Him in the dance, sing praises with the timbrel and harp, praise Him with the sound of the trumpet, the psaltery, stringed instruments, loud cymbals, high sounding instruments, the organ, by singing aloud in your beds, and by letting the high praises of God be in your mouth. According to the psalmist, "this honor has all the saints." It's an honor that we can praise the Lord.

There are times when it's hard to think of things to be thankful for because it seems like everything is a mess. But if we will start at the beginning—with trivial things—before long, we'll barely be able to keep up with all the things for which we are grateful. For instance, you may be tired of staying home or being sick in bed, but you could thank Him for a bed to sleep in . . . some people don't have one. You could thank Him for your life, your home, air conditioning, heat, a toilet, toilet paper (think of the importance of that for a minute), your furnace, food, shoes, clothes, flowers, trees, friends, family, and so on. Sometimes, we forget all of the wonderful, everyday blessings we have. Before long, your vision will change, and you will go from feeling depressed and bound to feeling blessed and free. Then, God can open your eyes to see and remember all He has truly done for you, blessed you with, and provided for you.

Let's challenge ourselves to stay in a place of praise—especially in these crazy days. Let's be intentional to see what He has done and is doing on our behalf. Praise Him for being our Savior, Provider, Healer, Deliverer, Comforter, Peace, Lord, our *all in all*. Praise Him, for He is truly worthy to be praised. Let's change our focus from our limitations to thanking God and praising Him. By doing so, I believe we can invite God to show up big time to do what only He can do.

Praise You, Lord! I give you glory and honor and I thank you for all of Your many blessings to be. You are worthy, Lord!

MY REFLECTION:

DAY 32
CONTINUE

COLOSSIANS 4:2
"Continue in prayer, and watch in the same with thanksgiving."

"Be earnest towards and be constantly diligent to pray to God in worship and with supplication and be vigilant to collect your thoughts, rise up again from your inactivity, and to keep awake in your praying with gratitude and thanksgiving to God." (NWI)

Wow, this packs a powerful punch in a few words!

The first thing this verse tells us is to "continue in prayer." In other words, keep on keeping on and don't quit! So many times, we can be easily frustrated with life, with a certain situation, a certain person, our physical health, or the health of a loved one. Somewhere along the way, we get tired and weary—we don't see anything happening, so we give up. The reality is, the answer might be right around the corner. Paul is encouraging us to be diligent to pray and not give up.

The word "prayer" as used in this verse means "prayer, worship, to pray earnestly, to pray to God." As we are earnestly lifting up our situations to God, we should include worship of who He is. Praise Him for His goodness. Thank Him for saving you. Thank Him for His blessings. Thank Him for whatever comes to your mind. Doing this changes the focus of the problem from *us* to *Him*. It builds our faith to believe for the answer. It gives us grateful hearts and reminds us that God is able to do "exceeding abundantly above all that we ask or think according to the power that worketh in us" (Ephesians 3:20).

Next, we see the word "watch," which in this verse refers to "keeping awake, being vigilant, being watchful, to rouse from sleep, sitting, disease or death, inactivity, to stand up." Paul is saying that, while we pray earnestly with worship, we should also be vigilant and "get off our duff." For me, there are definitely seasons in which my prayer life seems asleep or even dead—and still other seasons when I am earnestly praying for situations and people. There may be legitimate reasons for my lack of effort and limited prayer in any given season; nonetheless, my prayer life may not always be as effectual as it could be. But we plainly see in this passage the importance of not slacking in prayer. We must watchfully ensure that we don't give up before we see God answer our prayer request.

The word "thanksgiving" reflects what we saw with the word "prayer"—we should display a grateful heart to God. He appreciates the fact that we recognize His goodness to us. Once again, it changes our heart to see all God has done for us rather than to focus on the problem. It helps us to move past fear, anxiety, and worry to faith, hope, and encouragement.

Lord, help me to be diligent to pray, continuing, and not quitting, even when I don't see results right away. Help me to stay focused on what You have already done for me so that I can believe You for my next prayer need. I worship You for You alone are worthy of all praise.

MY REFLECTION:

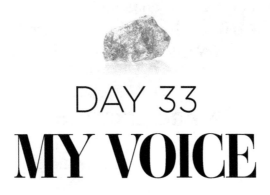

DAY 33
MY VOICE

PSALM 142:1

"I cried unto the LORD with my voice; with my voice
unto the LORD did I make my supplication."

*"I cried out in anguish as we gathered together and publicly called to
the self-existent and Eternal Lord with my thundering voice and yelling;
with my voice, I called aloud, to Jehovah Lord did I make my petition,
beseeching Him to move to favor me with His gracious mercy." (NWI)*

This passage reminds me of the people in the New Testament who cried out to Jesus for healing in the midst of the crowds. One such example is found in Mark 10:46-52, where we see the story of a blind man named Bartimaeus (son of Timaeus).

Bartimaeus was sitting by a highway begging people for money. When he heard Jesus was there, he "began to cry out, and say Jesus, thou son of David, have mercy on me." When many people told him to be quiet, he started yelling out even more for Jesus to have mercy on him. His action caused Jesus to literally stop in His tracks and stand still. Then, all the people telling him to be quiet were telling him Jesus was calling for him—that he should be cheerful and comforted.

The blind man actually threw off his garment so he could get up and go to Jesus. Jesus asked the blind man what he wanted Him to do for him, to which the blind man replied, "Lord, that I might receive my sight." Jesus told Bartimaeus that his faith, reliance, and assurance to believe was what made him whole. Immediately, blind Bartimaeus could see and he followed Jesus.

Verse 47 says that Bartimaeus did "cry out," meaning he croaked like a raven, screamed, or called aloud. In other words, he didn't care what he sounded like—that he wasn't proper. He gave everything he had to get Jesus's attention. Because of his faith and reliance on Christ, Jesus immediately healed him.

There may be someone telling you to shut up and quit. Are you willing to leave everything—even make a fool of yourself—to call out to God?

Lord, help me not to be so concerned about what others think.
Help me to be as bold the psalmist and as blind Bartimaeus—
to cry out to You in my desperation and need.

MY REFLECTION:

_____
_____
_____
_____
_____
_____
_____
_____
_____
_____
_____
_____
_____
_____
_____
_____
_____
_____
_____
_____
_____
_____

DAY 34
GIVING

2 CORINTHIANS 9:7

"Every man according as he purposeth in his heart, so let him give; not grudgingly, or of necessity; for God loveth a cheerful giver."

"Every man just as he chooses for himself as a preference, in his heart, thoughts, feelings, and mind, so let him give, not out of a place of sadness, grief, heaviness, or grudgingly, and not by means of distress, need, or constraint; for God has much love for a cheerful, willing, and hilarious giver who gives in averting some calamity in a prompt manner; it gives them power." (NWI)

One of the best ways to tell if a person is a Christian is how they spend their money. What is important to us is what we spend our money acquiring.

God has instructed us to tithe in many scripture references. Additionally, scripture encourages us to give offerings—extra giving—to help people or organizations that help others. For example, let's say you receive a check for $1,000. You would give $100 to your church before you pay any bills. After that, you might want to give some groceries to a family that's struggling or money to a ministry that helps with a specific need you feel is important.

But the biggest indicator of our faith with money is *how* we give it: "with cheer, willingly, and even hilariously giving" . . . or begrudgingly, feeling as if we *have* to give it. The Bible says God has much love when we do give with a cheerful heart, and by doing this, 2 Corinthians 9:7 says we are averting some calamity. Only God knows what that could be for each of us, but what an encouragement to know that He "has our back" when we are cheerful givers, obedient to His Word to tithe.

Lord, help me to realize that every cent of money I get is directly from You and I am only a steward of it. Help me, Lord, to be a cheerful giver.

MY REFLECTION:

DAY 35
WAY OF THE RIGHTEOUS

PROVERBS 15:19

"The way of the slothful man is as an hedge of thorns:
but the way of the righteous is made plain."

*"The road taken, course of life, and manner of an indolent, slothful
man is as a hedge of prickly thorns that restrains and shuts him
in: but the well-trodden road or highway of the upright is like
a turnpike and made plain for him to go down." (NWI)*

Slothful people are and will be very limited as to what they can do and where they can go. As a result of the person's lack of effort, "briars," "weeds," and "prickly thorny plants" have grown in a place that should have been tended to and cleared. Because slothful people don't take care of the "seeds" dropped by birds, blown by the wind, or scattered by squirrels, the plants that come up are going to restrict their life.

At first, this lack of effort won't cause too many problems, as the weeds and briars will be small and can be stepped over or on without much danger. If they are pulled up at this point, there won't be much pain involved. But because the slothful person doesn't exert much—if any—effort towards getting rid of the thorny plants or throwing out good seeds, the weeds will continue to grow. Eventually, they will overtake the entire area, making it difficult at best to get to a destination. There is no clear path to travel on, so an alternate route would need to be taken. Frequently, this causes loss of direction, resulting in these individuals giving up and turning back.

If, however, there is a righteous person willing to keep the path cleared out and tend to the unplanned scattered weeds and briars, there will be a well-maintained, easily-traveled road. Nothing will be restraining or prohibiting this person from journeying on that road whenever it is needed.

How does this apply to us spiritually? There are always going to be sins and temptations that come our way from unexpected sources. If we "tend" to those "seeds" right away, they will be easily removed—they won't "take root" in our lives, and we will be able to continue our walk with Jesus and go where He leads us. But if, when temptations come our way, we don't deal with them early on, they will take root in us, restrict us, and hinder our ability to walk on the path that otherwise could have been easily traveled.

The Lord has a purpose and plan for our lives that require us to walk down certain paths. Unless these paths are kept clean and cleared out, we won't be able to fulfill the callings on our lives. We will be restricted as to where we can go by the sins that have taken root and grown. But if we recognize the "thorny" plants and get rid of them early, we will have a clean, clear path to walk on to fulfill God's plans and purposes for our lives.

> Father, help me to always "keep my path clean." Show me areas in my life that are growing "thorny" plants so that I can clear them out. I want to walk the path that You have for me.

MY REFLECTION:

_____

_____

_____

_____

_____

_____

_____

_____

_____

_____

_____

_____

_____

_____

DAY 36
BLAMELESS

TITUS 1:7

"For a bishop must be blameless, as the steward of God; not self-willed, not soon angry, not given to wine, no striker, not given to filthy lucre."

"For a superintendent or Christian officer must be unaccused and
blameless, as the administrator of a religious economy of God:
not self-pleasing or arrogant, not soon angry with violent passion,
ire, or justifiable abhorrence, not staying near or given to wine,
not quarrelsome, nor being disgraceful or shameful." (NWI)

When we are in leadership, we are being watched by others. They see how we behave, how we govern our affairs—and those of the church—whether we depend on alcohol or other substances to get us through our troubles, or if we depend on the Lord. We all need to live our lives as if people are watching at all times, because they are! They want to see if what we say matches up with what we believe and how we act (or react). They want to know that being a follower of Jesus looks different than being of the world. They especially need and want to know that church leaders are able to depend on Jesus with their issues instead of being governed by their fleshly desires.

In our day-to-day lives, we all frequently face problems that stretch us to our boiling point. These may include dealings with your children, school, work, neighbors, spouse, friends, and so on. If we don't consistently turn our conversations, decisions, behaviors, and attitudes over to the Lord, asking for His help and direction, we may show sides of ourselves that don't glorify the Lord.

None of us are perfect, and we are always going to make mistakes, but the main thing is that we continually come before the Lord asking Him to lead us and help us. As we do, those in our spheres of influence will notice a difference between our response to things and their own. They will want to know what that difference is. Through this opportunity, you will be able to lead them in a saving knowledge of Jesus or help them to grow in their spiritual journey.

Someone is always paying attention to how you act and respond—whether it's your toddler, family members, neighbors, co-workers, people at the grocery store, or anyone else in your life. As leaders, we need to be aware of this fact. As we come across situations that stretch us emotionally, physically, mentally, or spiritually, our first thought should be to give it to the Lord so that He can lead us.

Lord, help me to reflect You to all who know me, watch me, and are around me. Let me not walk in my fleshly desires or actions, but instead in the strength and power You provide through Jesus and by the Spirit of God living in me.

MY REFLECTION:

_____

_____

_____

_____

_____

_____

_____

_____

_____

_____

_____

_____

_____

_____

_____

_____

_____

_____

_____

_____

_____

DAY 37

RESIST TEMPTATIONS

2 CHRONICLES 12:14

"And he did evil, because he prepared not his heart to seek the Lord."

God warns us in this passage that, if we don't prepare our hearts to seek the Lord, it can cause us to sin, which is evil in the Lord's eyes. But how do we do this? How can we prepare our hearts to seek the Lord?

The main way is spending time with Him in His Word and in prayer. Prayer is simply talking with God and letting Him know what's on our hearts. If we spend time reading or hearing the Word of God and praying, it will help us refrain from sinning and restrain our fleshly desires. If we know what God's Word says about various issues of life—what pleases or displeases the Lord—we will be more apt to obey His Word. When we are faced with temptations—whether they are as simple as lying or being in fear, or more cynical, like murder—we will know what is pleasing to our Father and be able to draw near to Him instead of the sin. If, however, we haven't prepared our hearts to seek God by reading His Word and praying, when temptations come, we will more easily fall into their snares.

This topic reminds me of the "tornado drills" we all did in school. About once a month, an alarm would go off. We were to quickly, quietly, and calmly line up, go into the hallway and walk to our appointed location, sit on the floor with our heads covered with our hands, and stay there until we were told that everything was clear. Since we practiced ahead of time, when or if the emergency arose, we were more readily able to deal with the disaster because we were prepared. We knew what to do and what not to do.

The same principle applies with seeking the Lord before you are tempted. Instead of waiting until something happens and then seeking God, we need to read our Bibles daily, pray continually, and seek the Lord. Then, we will be prepared when temptations come. The Lord is always ready and willing to listen to our prayers, and He is faithful to hear our cries of help.

Father, I earnestly desire to seek You first in my life and to be prepared by reading Your Word and praying so that, when I am tempted to sin against You, I will be able to resist the temptation.

MY REFLECTION:

DAY 38
STAND FAST

GALATIANS 5:1
"Stand fast therefore in the liberty wherewith Christ hath made us free, and be not entangled again with the yoke of bondage."

"Persevere and stand fast accordingly in the liberty and freedom of a citizen by which Christ, the anointed Messiah has delivered and made us free, and don't keep a grudge, have a quarrel against or become ensnared again, repeating it anew by joining or coupling yourself with obligations and thus become a slave in bondage." (NWI)

Just like our country has had to stand fast at various times against other countries to maintain our freedom, we as Christians must also persevere and stand fast in the liberty, freedom, and deliverance Jesus has freely provided for us.

Some of the many tools for keeping our personal freedom include not holding grudges, quarreling, or doing "what we used to do." Not forgiving others, holding grudges, arguing, and sinning is what put us in bondage before, and it's what will put us back into bondage again.

I would much rather live free of guilt, fear, anxiety, hopelessness, and shame. Call me crazy, but living without those things makes life so much more enjoyable. I'm no longer bound up and restricted. Jesus paid for you and me to live victoriously in Him, and He provides peace, joy, hope, love, patience, and all of the fruit of the Spirit to abide in us so that we will live a better life and enjoy each other. I want to walk in that freedom, and I hope you do too.

Lord, help me to walk in the fullness You have so graciously provided for me. Help me not to fall back into my old habits, lifestyles, or the things that held me in bondage before. Instead, help me live in the provision of Your grace, mercy, peace, purpose, and all that You have for me.

MY REFLECTION:

DAY 39
GOD'S LOVINGKINDNESS

PSALM 48:9

"We have thought of thy lovingkindness, O God, in the midst of thy temple."

T he word "temple" in this passage more than likely refers to a literal building where God dwells; but according to 1 Corinthians 3:16 ("Don't you know that you are the temple of God, and that the Spirit of God dwells in you?"), it could also refer to us. Either way, whether we are in church or by ourselves, it is important to think of and remember the Lord's lovingkindnesses to us.

As we remember the many times and ways in which God has helped us through our struggles and shown His lovingkindness and faithfulness to us, we need to share those examples with others. We should think of His provision, wisdom, direction, guidance, love, salvation, forgiveness, healing, hope, protection, deliverance, and everything else He has done for us. When we do, it helps us believe for future situations that we may encounter—whether for ourselves or for others.

This remembrance reminds us that He did it before, so He can do it again. It will build our faith, help us to endure, strengthen our character, and encourage us. By thinking of God's lovingkindness to us, we will remember His faithfulness, His comfort, and His doing something for us that no one knew about—something no one else could do. By reflecting on how the Lord has been kind to us, we will know how to better love and be kind to others.

If we think on those things, we will be more apt to believe His Word, trust Him, help others, show the love of Christ to those who need Him, and teach others kindness (which is desperately needed today).

Father, I pray I would be ever-mindful of Your lovingkindnesses to me. Help me to reflect on them so I can better understand how You love and how You are kind. Help me display that love and kindness to others.

MY REFLECTION:

DAY 40
WWJD

ROMANS 1:16

"For I am not ashamed of the gospel of Christ: for it is the power of God unto salvation to every one that believeth; to the Jew first, and also to the Greek."

Back in the 90s, it was popular to wear various articles of clothing with the slogan, "What Would Jesus Do?" There were t-shirts, bracelets, and sweatshirts with WWJD emblazoned on them. I used to have a t-shirt with these words in large letters.

I was teaching in a local public school at the time, and it had become a Friday tradition to have "casual Friday," in which we were allowed to wear jeans, t-shirts, sweatshirts, and more casual clothing. On June 5, 1998, I wore my WWJD shirt to school, which was much more obvious than my typical way of making sure everyone knew I was a Christian. Early on that particular day, I was called into the principal's office, a trip for which the assistant principal walked behind me. Boy, did I think I must have done something wrong—it required both of them to talk to me. Yikes!

As it turned out, I wasn't in trouble at all. On the contrary, they called me to the office to let me know that my husband had been in an accident at work. Now, Jim had warned me our entire 26 years of married life of what could happen if there was an accident at work and what to do if one occurred. I was quite aware of the seriousness of the situation. To make matters worse, while I was sitting in the principal's office, a tornado went down the road we were on, the electricity went out in the school, and the phones went out as well (this was before cell phones were popular).

There I was, sitting in the principal's office, knowing something serious had happened to my husband. I couldn't get any information, I couldn't leave to go to the hospital, the principal was trying to take care of the 700-plus students and staff, and—again—there was no electricity. I was scared on so many levels, anxiously wanting to get to the hospital but not being able to leave. I didn't know what to do.

Finally, things cleared up weather-wise, and the principal was able to drive me down to the hospital, where I found out that my husband had passed away about three hours prior. So many thoughts were rushing through my mind. I collapsed onto the floor after the doctor told me they had done everything they could, including resuscitating him twice. He had been smashed between two railroad cars—thankfully, you couldn't see any injuries from his chest upward.

I was keenly aware that day—as friends and family members came by the hospital and to our home to be with me and pay their respects—of the message I was wearing. Some of the people there were not Christians, and I knew they would be "watching me" to see if having Jesus in my life made a difference. It reminded me that I needed to reflect Jesus in my life even in the midst of the most difficult of circumstances.

People need to know there is a hope and peace we can have, no matter how hard life gets. I'm not going to pretend I didn't cry, get upset, mourn, or grieve; but in and through it all, as I sought the Lord, He gave me His peace that passes understanding, His strength in my weakness, His beauty for my ashes, His help when I lacked understanding or wisdom, and His faithfulness when things seemed to be amiss.

Sometimes, we might need that reminder while we're going through difficult times. 1 Thessalonians 1:3, 5 says, "Remembering without ceasing your work of faith, and labour of love, and patience of hope in our Lord Jesus Christ, in the sight of God and our Father . . . For our gospel came not unto you in word only, but also in power, and in the Holy Ghost, and in much assurance; as you know what manner of men we were among you for your sake."

Father, help me to be Your example to others around me, letting them know You are faithful to take care of me no matter how difficult my situation. Help me fall into Your arms of love, grace, compassion, and mercy, trusting You for every need I have. Help me to live my life as a reflection of Your faithfulness to me.

MY REFLECTION:

_____

_____

_____

_____

_____

_____

_____

_____

DAY 41
LIFTING OUR HANDS

PSALM 63:4

"Thus will I bless thee while I live: I will lift up my hands in thy name."

D avid said that the way he would bless the Lord was to lift up his hands unto the Lord. It's interesting that one of the hardest things for people to do is lift their hands to the Lord. It is an act of surrender and worship to God.

During worship, people will stand and sing in church, but frequently have a hard time giving themselves to the Lord by surrendering their will and raising their hands in submission and honor. They'll lift their hands, shout, and show honor to famous people—whether entertainers, athletes, politicians, or other celebrities—but they struggle when it comes to raising their hands to praise and honor the Lord.

During the Third Reich, Adolf Hitler made his people lift their right arm as they walked by him, and would require them to say, "Heil Hitler," meaning *hail Hitler*. When the police capture someone, they ask the person to lift their hands in the air, which is a way of surrendering to authority and letting the police officer know that the person isn't going to try to fight back. When we lift our hands in the name of the Lord, we are saying to Him, "I surrender to Your authority," "You are worthy to be praised," "I am honoring You," or, "I am letting You be in charge." You are letting the Lord know that you are reverencing and trusting Him.

You definitely don't have to raise your hands to worship the Lord; but when you do, there is an unexplainable freedom that occurs. Freedom comes because you are giving yourself and all of your circumstances to Him and allowing Him to be in control instead of you trying to take care of everything.

I challenge you to try it. Try lifting your hands in honor and praise to the Lord. I can personally testify to the fact that, whenever I raise my hands in worship, it brings joy, peace, and freedom to me. It doesn't even have to be high in the air—it just needs to be an acknowledgment that you have surrendered yourself and your problems to Him. When we do so, God's Word says that it actually blesses the Lord. Wow! I sure do want to be a blessing to the Lord—I hope you do too.

> Father, forgive me for the times I haven't submitted myself
> to You by surrendering and lifting my hands to You. I pray I
> would always remain humble before You and acknowledge
> Your Lordship by raising my hands in Your name.

MY REFLECTION:

_____

_____

_____

_____

_____

_____

_____

_____

_____

_____

_____

_____

_____

_____

_____

_____

_____

_____

_____

_____

_____

DAY 42
WATCH

COLOSSIANS 4:2

"Continue in prayer, and watch in the same with thanksgiving."

"You be earnest, constantly diligent, and persevere, continuing in worship and prayer, and be vigilant and watchful in yourself together with gratitude and thankfulness." (NWI)

God calls us to be "constantly diligent" in worship and prayer. Some of the best times I've had with the Lord have been when I am in worship and prayer—not just prayer. Prayer is good, and we need to "pray without ceasing" as Paul tells us in 1 Thessalonians 5:17; but to include our worship to the Father in our prayers puts them on another level of intimacy.

Psalm 100:4 says to "enter into his gates with thanksgiving, and into his courts with praise." To enter into the very court of God, we must come with praise in our hearts and on our lips. John 9:31 says, "Now we know that God doesn't hear sinners: but if any man be a worshipper of God, and does his will, him he heareth." If you want God to hear your prayers, come in "worship and prayer." But notice that Colossians 4:2 also tells us to be "earnest, constantly diligent, persevere, continuing." This is a decision on our part to keep doing it and not stop worshipping and praying, whether in good times or bad—to worship God, even when things don't make sense. That's when our faith, hope, confidence, trust, and peace comes—when we believe God no matter what we see with our eyes or hear with our ears. It's that place where we can rest in the confidence that "God has this!"

The last part of the verse says to be "vigilant and watch in yourself." Again, this indicates a decision on our part. If we don't "watch in ourselves," we will quit, get distracted, get busy, lose sight, or forget to continue to be earnest and diligent. Let's ever strive to worship the Lord and acknowledge His greatness, power, faithfulness, and authority so that we can release our burdens and cares to Him.

Father, I worship You today because You are God, the Maker of heaven and earth, the Almighty God, the Everlasting Father. You are worthy of all praise, Lord. There is none like You. In You we live, breathe, and have our being. Thank You, Lord, for Your faithfulness to us.

MY REFLECTION:

DAY 43
GOD'S GOODNESS

NUMBERS 6:24-26, 27b

"The LORD bless thee, and keep thee: the LORD make his face shine upon thee, and be gracious unto thee: the LORD lift up his countenance upon thee, and give thee peace . . . and I will bless them."

"The Lord abundantly praise, bless and congratulate you, and protect, regard and hedge you about: The Lord make His countenance, favor, and presence be like the break of day, making a luminous, shining above, among, beside and touching you, and to favor, be merciful, stoop in kindness as to an inferior and have pity on you. The Lord bring forth His countenance, favor, and presence to ease, forgive, change, and pardon you, to purposely reward and wholly give you safety, happiness, health, prosperity, perfect peace, and welfare . . . and I will abundantly bless, praise and congratulate them." (NWI)

This amazing prayer and blessing that many pastors declare over their congregations is full of meaning. We need to understand the importance of what is actually being said over us.

Firstly, we can actually have God's praise and congratulations as His child, just like an earthly father would praise his child. Secondly, we can have God's protection like a hedge around us. Then, it says we can have God's favor and presence in our lives that shines like the break of day. Next, we can have God's mercy and pity. The Lord's countenance and presence will ease us, forgive us, change us, reward us, give us happiness, safety, health, prosper us, and give us His perfect peace. Lastly, the passage ends like it began, with the fact that the Lord will abundantly bless and praise us.

The next time a pastor or anyone else speaks this blessing over you, receive what is being declared, because it is full of God's goodness towards us His children.

Lord, thank You for all that You provide for us, Your children.

MY REFLECTION:

DAY 44

WITHSTANDING THE STORM

HEBREWS 4:16

"Let us therefore come boldly unto the throne of grace, that we may obtain mercy, and find grace to help in time of need."

"Let us accordingly approach, come near, and worship with all outspokenness, frankness, and confidence to come boldly to the power and throne of the divine influence on our heart and its reflection in our life of acceptance, favor, joy, and liberality, that we may get hold of, obtain and receive God's and human compassion and tender mercy, and find, perceive, and obtain acceptance, favor, joy, grace, and liberality to help us by putting a rope, strap, or chain under us to keep us from falling apart when it is an opportune time of need." (NWI)

In old times, when a boat was in danger of sinking, the crew would strap ropes or chains around the hull to keep it from falling apart. With this added support, the boat would have a good chance of surviving the stormy water.

God can shore up our lives in order to withstand any storm. He doesn't remove us from the storms of life but rather gives us the grace and mercy to withstand them. He will not allow you to be tested beyond your power to remain firm. At the time you are tested, if you confidently come to the throne of God's grace, He will give you the strength to endure it and provide you with a way to get through the storm's darkness and chaos.

As we do this, others will see how His compassion, favor, acceptance, and tender mercy have brought us through something that would normally break us apart. Not only does God help us through the difficulties of life when we worship Him, but He also uses those situations to draw others to Himself. Those around us will see the difference that trusting the Lord makes in our lives.

They will be able to see that, when the trials of life come our way, we depend on the One who can prevent us from "sinking," and we are able to weather the storm.

This doesn't mean there won't be storms, or that they won't throw things our way; but it does mean God will provide the protection, wisdom, and help we need to get to the other side.

Lord, thank You for always being there for me when I go through the storms of life. Thank You that You are faithful to "shore" me up so I remain intact when difficulties come my way. Help me to always go to You first instead of allowing the fear of the storm to break me apart. I know I can always trust You to do what is best for me.

MY REFLECTION:

DAY 45
FOR A PURPOSE

GENESIS 2:7

"And the LORD God formed man of the dust of the ground . . . "

"And the Lord God molded and squeezed into shape like a potter for and with a purpose, man, of the clay of the earth. . . ." (NWI)

I love this verse! We are all made by the God that created the whole universe, and everything in it, with and for a purpose! We were not made by accident, or because He "had an idea." He has a purpose for each one of us.

Some people really need to take hold of that statement. Just like a potter has something in mind when he forms a piece of pottery, God had you and me in mind when He created us. He made each of us unique for a reason. We were created, molded, and squeezed to be who we are. Who we are is a decision He made.

If that wasn't enough, He made us with a purpose—there is something we were designed to do. My husband and I both love pottery, so we enjoy going to art festivals or galleries to see the beautiful pieces various potters make. I am always intrigued by the creativity of some of the pieces. Each is beautifully made, each with a specific purpose, each with its own unique colors or patterns, and each was directly held in the potter's hands. There are many artists that design the same basic piece, with the same basic-colored glazes, and they basically all look alike. But there are some that are so special that you can tell the artist spent extra time molding, shaping, painting, firing, and cooling them.

That's us! Each of us is like that special piece that has been given extra attention and made uniquely. God has given each of us a purpose. Pottery pieces fall under different categories, such as bowls, cups, platters, soap dishes, spoon rests, or décor items—each with their own uses. Let's not forget that God also has a purpose and plan for each of us and He uses us with that purpose in mind. He has uniquely designed us with special gifts and talents that make us different than anyone else. We may all have the same basic purpose, but God made each of us to fulfill that purpose in a way different than anyone else.

We have individual ways of doing things that enable us to reach others with our own distinct gifts. God took extra special care to make each of us just the way He did, with all of the character, color, design, shape, and purpose needed to make us who we are.

Father, thank You for making me uniquely different from anyone else. Thank You that You made me with a specific purpose. Help me, Lord, to recognize what You created me to do so that I can operate in that purpose.

MY REFLECTION:

DAY 46
LOOK DILIGENTLY

HEBREWS 12:15

"Looking diligently lest any man fail of the grace of God; lest any root of bitterness springing up trouble you, and thereby many be defiled."

"Be aware, look diligently, investigate, and seek after in worship, whether any man be inferior, be deficient, lack, or be the worse of the divine (godly) influence upon the heart; neither any root of pressing down or apprehension be germinated and grow to crowd you in, troubling and annoying you and because of that, many be contaminated and defiled." (NWI)

"Y ou" is inferred in this verse—as in *"you* be aware, *you* look diligently, *you* investigate, *you* seek after the Lord in worship." It is our responsibility to be watchful as to who or what we allow around us, because those things can cause not only ourselves to be affected, but others around us to be defiled as well.

If we are not careful, we can take on others' bitterness, anger, and resentments and pass them to others around us. For example, let's say you have a friend going through a difficult time at work. Their boss has been harassing them, and they come to you for advice as to how to handle the situation. The whole conversation, if turned over to the Lord for wisdom, can be dealt with healthily—your friend will be encouraged as to how to handle the situation.

But if it's not handled correctly, not only will your friend resent their boss, but you will, as well. This can lead you to see things differently at your workplace, causing you to feel differently towards your boss—even though before, there were no issues. If you don't turn it over to the Lord, you can take on your friend's bitterness and make it your own. Since you are now acting differently towards your boss, you no longer have the favor you once did, adding even more "fuel to the fire." Your co-workers may act differently now because you've started spreading "gossip" that isn't true. Instead of having a peaceful, caring workplace, you are now in an environment that breeds dissension strife, envy, and disrespect.

All of this can be avoided if we heed this scripture. Of course, this can also apply to our home situations, our families, and our churches. If we don't turn over to the Lord the issues and the people in our lives, we can easily take on their problems, hurts, and pain. Not only will this affect our lives—it will also filter down to those around us. We must be ever-mindful to seek after the Lord so that other's issues don't become ours. Let's let the Lord handle them, and leave them at His footstool.

Father, help me to seek You first in every situation. Help me not to take on others' problems to the point that they become an issue for me. When someone comes to me for guidance or prayer, help me to give it all to You, seek Your wisdom, forgive, and show love.

MY REFLECTION:

DAY 47
TITHING

MALACHI 3:10-11

"Bring ye all the tithes into the storehouse, that there may be meat in mine house, and prove me now herewith, saith the LORD of hosts, if I will not open you the windows of heaven, and pour you out a blessing, that there shall not be room enough to receive it. And I will rebuke the devourer for your sakes, and he shall not destroy the fruits of your ground; neither shall your vine cast her fruit before the time in the field, saith the LORD of hosts."

If we are obedient to tithe to the Lord, to prove Him, He will open the windows of heaven to pour out gigantic blessings. Not only that, but He will rebuke the devil for us so that he can't destroy the fruits of our ground and so that our fruit will not fall off of the vine before it's ripe. In both situations, it's the Lord of hosts that declares this; the One who has the host of His angelic army to fight for Him.

Tithing is giving the first ten percent of our income to the Lord. It is bringing to your house of worship (church) your "first fruits." God shows us this principle throughout His Word, but in essence, it is honoring God with your best and first. In this verse, we see that we need to bring our tithes to church so that God can use it to help others, not just to build a bigger and better facility.

Also, by giving God the first of your income, you're telling Him that you trust Him and honor Him. Not only will He bless the ninety percent of your money that's left, but verse 10 says He will actually open up the windows of heaven to pour out such a blessing that we won't even have room enough to receive it. He will multiply that ninety percent to be more than enough—plus throw in some more. I have no idea how He does it, but I can attest to the fact that He does.

I've seen Him take a meager amount of money in my checkbook and make it last to pay all of the bills. I'll start opening bills to find that the company didn't send a bill, but simply some information. When I thought I would have eight bills in front of me, I would open the envelopes to find only three. One time, I had a whole stack of envelopes I dreaded opening, only to find that none were bills. Sometimes, I'd be so amazed I wouldn't even know what to say except to thank and praise Him.

It may not always be monetary blessings—God is not limited in how He can bless us. It might come through people giving you gift cards, or receiving coupons for a restaurant, friends being willing to help you move, saving you the cost of paying for movers, and so on. God honors His Word. He tells us to prove or test Him in this principle because He wants to show us that He can and will do it for us. He is faithful!

Being obedient to tithe is so important that God uses His angel armies to bring His promise to pass on our behalf. In other words, if the devil is trying to "steal" from you and take your money by various means, if you will continue to tithe and honor the Lord, He will literally rebuke the devil and do whatever it takes to show you His faithfulness in this promise. It makes no sense, but you can count on God to do what He tells us in His Word concerning tithing.

Father, help me to be faithful in honoring You with the first of my money. I know that, as I give You what is already Yours, You will show Your faithfulness to Your promise in Malachi 3:10-11 to bless the ninety percent that is left. Thank You for Your Word and for providing for me as I trust You with the money over which You have allowed me to be steward. Help me to always be a good steward over Your blessings to me.

MY REFLECTION:

_____

_____

_____

_____

_____

_____

_____

_____

_____

_____

_____

_____

_____

DAY 48
LOVE ONE ANOTHER

1 PETER 2:1-2

"Wherefore laying aside all malice, and all guile, and hypocrisies, and envies, and all evil speakings. as newborn babes, desire the sincere milk of the word, that ye may grow thereby."

Peter is writing to the "strangers scattered throughout Pontus, Galatia, Cappadocia, Asia, and Bithynia" (1 Peter 1:1) who were "elect" (1 Peter 1:2) and telling them to "be ye holy in all manner of conversation" (behavior) (1 Peter 1:15), "because it is written, Be ye holy; for I am holy." (verse 16), because "ye were . . . redeemed" (vs. 18) "with the precious blood of Christ" (verse 19). The first chapter goes on, "Seeing ye have purified your souls in obeying the truth through the Spirit unto unfeigned love of the brethren, see that ye love one another with a pure heart fervently: Being born again" (22-23a).

If we choose to love one another rather than trying to deceive, slander, be jealous, show spite, or condemn others, we will grow up spiritually into men and women of God. But if we continue to put people down, speak evil of others, do evil, or try to deceive people, we will remain a "baby" spiritually. Jeremiah 9:6 says, "Thine habitation is in the midst of deceit; through deceit they refuse to know me, saith the LORD." The Spirit of God can help us, but we must make the conscious decision to allow Him to help us in our weak moments. Peter told his audience they needed to "lay aside" all manner of evil—it was a decision they had to make not to do those things, to instead choose to love and be holy. We can choose to be Christ-like . . . or not. Let's choose to show love to others like God shows to us.

God's word is rational and reasonable. When we choose to follow love, we are acting out of a rational and reasonable mindset rather than choosing to do evil against others, which always ends in non-rational or unreasonable action. We see society today dealing with "road rage," choosing to fight, becoming angry instantly, and hurting or killing others rather than showing God's love, which brings forgiveness, kindness, and understanding.

Especially as Christians, our focus needs to be on what God would have us do, not on how our flesh wants to respond. Things are going to happen—people are going to mess up and even hurt us. We can choose not to respond in kind, but instead to walk in love. As we do, we will grow and mature into men and women of God.

Lord, I pray I would follow after Your love, forgiveness, kindness, and understanding rather than my natural feelings. Help me show others what You have extended to me so graciously.

MY REFLECTION:

DAY 49
DON'T BE OBLIVIOUS

PSALM 103:1-3

"Bless the Lord, O my soul: and all that is within me, bless his holy name. Bless the Lord, O my soul, and forget not all his benefits: who forgiveth all thine iniquities; who healeth all thy diseases."

"Abundantly bless in adoration, praise, and thank the Lord, O my breath, mind, desire, and soul, and all that is within and pertains to me, bless His hallowed name of authority. Bless the Lord, O my breath, mind, desire, and soul, and don't mislay, be oblivious of because you aren't paying attention or forget all His acts of good, benefits, rewards, and those things He has given you. Who forgives, pardons, and spares all your faults, perversities, moral evils or sins: Who mends by stitching, cures, causes to heal, repairs, and thoroughly makes whole, all your maladies, sicknesses, and diseases." (NWI)

I have a friend who said, "Wow, that covers everything!" It pretty much does, doesn't it?

Upon looking at the fulness of what God is telling us as expressed in the NWI, I was totally struck by the part that says, "don't mislay, be oblivious of because you weren't paying attention, or forget." I wonder how many blessings, rewards, benefits, and good things God has done for us that we were oblivious to because we weren't paying attention. I wonder how many we forgot about or didn't give credit to God for after the fact. He is always looking out for our good, protecting us, providing for us, and yet we—or maybe I should just say I—don't always recognize some of His benefits toward us.

Possibly, my mind is elsewhere, thinking on other things, worrying about people or circumstances, or just not paying attention. But in these verses is the fact that it is a decision, a choice, a conscious act on my part to give God praise, adoration, and thanks for what He has done for me.

Even if He didn't do one other thing than forgive my sins and save me (which He has done, along with so much more), He deserves my constant praise and appreciation.

Just like the amazing God that He is, though, He goes much further than providing forgiveness and salvation through Jesus Christ. He heals, makes whole, mends, and even stitches together my messes, my body, my feelings, my hurts, my emotions, and everything else that pertains to me. If I constantly choose to look for all of His benefits, I truly believe I will be overwhelmed with His goodness.

Father, I pray I would be especially aware and overcome with what You did for us on the cross in the death and resurrection of Jesus. I pray that my heart, mind, emotions, and soul would "bless the Lord," for You are truly worthy to be praised.

MY REFLECTION:

_____

_____

_____

_____

_____

_____

_____

_____

_____

_____

_____

_____

_____

_____

_____

_____

_____

DAY 50
NIGHT STUMBLES

JOHN 11:10

"But if a man walk in the night, he stumbleth, because there is no light in him."

When we walk around the house at night with no lights on, it's easy to stumble over or into things. We can't see where we're going and what's in our path. But when the lights are on, we can easily navigate around obstacles, whether they be furniture, toys, shoes, walls, or whatever. How much easier it is to see where we are going when we turn on a light—not to mention safer!

It's the same thing spiritually speaking. If we try to "walk," "move," or "work," without the light of Jesus to clearly guide us, there's a good chance we'll stumble, run into something, get hurt, fall, or go the wrong way. It is better to "rest" during those times, until we have "the light of Jesus" on the matter. In other words, it is better to wait patiently for God to lead us rather than trying to do something without His direction. In essence, the latter is like walking in the dark. Sometimes, it is tempting to do whatever we feel pressed to do; but in actuality, we would navigate better and more quickly if our "light" was on. Without God's direction, we are stumbling, going in wrong directions, and possibly even getting hurt because we can't see clearly.

But how do we "turn on" God's light? Firstly, if you haven't already done so, you need to ask Jesus to be your Lord and Savior. It's very simple, really. Ask Him to forgive you of your sins and come into your heart. Surrender to Him. When you do this, He can and will help you with your life and your decisions. You don't have to say all kinds of words, unless you have more you want to say to Him. It's that easy!

After you have done that, you can read your Bible, which is God speaking to us and telling us how we should live our best lives. Sometimes, you may have questions that God's Word doesn't talk about, like, *Which job should I take? What car should I buy? What college should I go to?* In these cases, you can pray (talk to Him) and ask Him what you should do.

I have found that the Holy Spirit will lead me as to what I need to do. *How?* you might want to know? It will be that still, small voice that some people recognize as a gut feeling. Sometimes,

He'll use a person or situation as confirmation for what you are to do. Still other times, the answer will come from His Word. No matter how He speaks to or directs you, it is always better to do what He's telling you to do. Your path will be clearly lit and there won't be any stumbling about.

If we are "in the dark" about something spiritually, it is better to just wait until "the lights come on" before we try to move forward.

How can those who are blind and can never see get where they are going? Usually, if they are in an unfamiliar place, they have someone to walk with them and lead them to avoid running into problems, going the wrong way, or getting hurt. Jesus is that for us. He leads us, guides us through obstacles, and helps us safely get to where we need to be.

Father, I ask You right now to show me what I need to do or where I need to be. I pray that Your light would shine brightly for me to see what is best. Clearly, make Yourself known and lead me into Your righteousness.

MY REFLECTION:

DAY 51
GOD'S GIFTS

JUDGES 16:5

"And the lords of the Philistines came up unto her, and said unto her, Entice him, and see wherein his great strength lieth, and by what means we may prevail against him, that we may bind him to afflict him: and we will give thee every one of us eleven hundred pieces of silver."

Samson knew that he was a Nazarite, and that God did miracles through him, but he didn't seem to have a heart knowledge and true understanding of these truths. If he did, he would have submitted his gifts and callings to the Lord so that God could get the glory.

Like Samson, it is important that we are careful with whom we join in friendship and marriage. Though Samson trusted Delilah and possibly even loved her, she apparently did not share these feelings. It appears she was only interested in Samson so she could get money from the Philistine lords. Samson allowed his fleshly desires to blind him (spiritually) to the truth, which ultimately led to his being physically blinded.

The lords were using Delilah and Delilah was using Samson. Had Samson not been led by his flesh but rather allowed the Lord to lead him, God could have used him mightily for His kingdom. Instead of trusting the Lord, he trusted in the women he gave himself to physically, mentally, emotionally, and spiritually. The weakness of his sin (his flesh) caused him to become spiritually weak. He knew his strength came from the Lord, but rather than allowing God to show him how to rightly use that strength, he operated in his own understanding and used his strength for his own glory.

This story reminds me of various men and women of God who are used by the Lord to heal, deliver, and lead people to Jesus—but because they have not surrendered their anointings to the Lord, they are not as effective as God would desire. Just like Samson saw God's hand upon his life for miracles, modern-day people do as well; but because they do not surrender and submit their callings to the Lord, they are never able to do all God has planned, thus frustrating them.

We need to ask ourselves who we are allowing to take away the gifts and blessings God has given us. Who do we relinquish ourselves to (surrender ourselves to) other than God? What fleshly desires are we allowing to govern our lives? What gift(s) that God has given us to be used for His kingdom and glory are we wasting? What is blinding us from seeing God's truth? Who are we trusting more than God? Who or what is deceiving us to do or believe something that is not from the Lord?

Deep down, I know what my calling is, but my insecurities sometimes get the better of me. Sure, there are legitimate reasons for my insecurities, but nonetheless, my faith and trust should be in the Lord and not in people's opinions, which have caused me to doubt what God has given me to do or say. Just like Samson, I sometimes allow others and their opinions to lead and guide me rather than trusting what I believe the Lord has spoken to me about a particular situation.

How are you being affected? Once you recognize that you are allowing others to rob you of what God has put in you to do for His kingdom, you need to repent, as I have, and give your gifts and calling back to Him to use.

Lord, I pray that You would forgive me for allowing others to lead me away from trusting You regarding my calling. Help me to recognize Your voice. Help me to have my eyes open to see, my ears open to hear, and my heart open to understand Your calling in my life. Lord, let me not be deceived by the lusts of my flesh.

MY REFLECTION:

DAY 52
SETTLING

1 KINGS 18:21

"And Elijah came unto all the people, and said, How long halt ye
between two opinions? If the Lord be God, follow him."

I wonder how many times we have settled for less than God's best because we quit, gave up too soon, didn't trust the Lord or, worse yet, never accepted Jesus as our Lord.

As I was studying Elijah, I came across a verse that reminded me of this. To do a quick recap, King Ahab (Jezebel's husband) had caused the people of Israel to abandon their faith in God and serve Baal. It was so bad God told Elijah to declare that if they didn't submit to the Lord, there would be no rain for three-and-a-half years (yikes!). God did some miracles along the way to provide for Elijah during this time, using him to provide food and water for a widow, her son, and her household.

Things were getting really bad in the land, however—a lack of rain caused a famine. King Ahab decided he needed to be sure his horses and mules were cared for, so he told a follower of God that worked for him named Obadiah to help him find some water and grass for his livestock. 1 Kings 18:5 says, "And Ahab said unto Obadiah, Go into the land, unto all fountains of water, and unto all brooks: peradventure we may find grass to save the horses and mules alive, that we lose not all the beasts."

We see here that Ahab is settling. Given the circumstances of not having rain for more than three years, Ahab was trying to figure out a way to save his livestock. Seems logical, right? You may ask, *Why is that settling?* If Ahab and the people had followed the Lord, there wouldn't have been lack of rain or the resulting famine. Instead, there would have been blessing. But rather than surrender to the Living God, he "settled" by trying to save some of his animals the only way he knew how.

How does this apply to us? Instead of waiting on the promises God has for us, we go ahead of Him to try to "make it happen." We're doing our best to "make do" when, if we would trust the Lord in the first place, He would provide "exceeding abundantly above all that we ask or think" (Ephesians 3:20). Settling usually requires "jumping the gun" or doing something in our own understanding, being afraid of what might happen if we don't, and trying to figure out problems on our own. It's not trusting the Lord or committing the issues to Him; it's not surrendering our time, life, problems, talents, hurts, concerns, limitations, and circumstances.

Settling could include things like not waiting for the Lord's spouse but settling on someone just so you won't be alone anymore; taking a job you don't like because you're afraid a better one won't come along; buying the first house you can because you're tired of renting; and the list goes on. Settling for a Christian is not waiting for God's best for us but trying to make it happen on our own. But if we would surrender our concerns to Jesus and wait patiently for His timing, we might find out that we "can do all things through Christ" (Philippians 4:13), have all of our needs met (Philippians 4:19), and can have "love, joy, peace, longsuffering, gentleness, goodness, faith, meekness, temperance" (Galatians 5:22).

In and of ourselves, we are limited; but with the God of possibilities as our Lord, nothing is impossible. Sometimes, the answers may be different than we may desire at the time, but if we will "seek ye first the kingdom of God, and His righteousness; and all things shall be added unto you" (Matthew 6:33). We don't seek the provision, we seek the Provider—and we will see that "all things work together for good" (Romans 8:28). Settling is never as good as God wants us to have as His children.

Father, teach me to patiently wait on You rather than trying to do things in my way and my timing. Help me not to try to make things happen by settling for second best, when You have something better for me that I might not understand yet.

MY REFLECTION:

_____

_____

_____

_____

_____

_____

_____

_____

_____

_____

_____

_____

DAY 53
COMPASSION

I PETER 3:8

"Finally, be ye all of one mind, having compassion one of another, love as brethren, be pitiful, be courteous:"

"The conclusion of it all and the point at which you aim for, is that you should be harmonious and of one mind, having sympathy and compassion to one another, loving people as if they were brothers, being humane and courteous, you need to be well compassioned, sympathetic and tenderhearted, and you need to be kind, courteous and friendly." (NWI)

In this verse, following his instructions to husbands and wives, Peter describes how we should treat one another. I have to believe he was still talking about spouses here, but this passage also extends to everyone who comes into contact with us. What if we were using this verse in our lives as a model when someone "did us wrong"?

What if, when someone was rude, treated us unkindly, didn't acknowledge us, or did or said something they shouldn't, instead of showing "road rage," anger, hurt, or resentment, we tried to understand that that person may be dealing with something? What if we understood that they're hurting, which is why they acted the way they did? What if we extended sympathy, compassion, love, kindness, friendliness, or courtesy instead of what our flesh feels like doing?

I wonder what God would do in our lives—and theirs—if we operated by this verse instead of taking the position of retaliation? Jude 22 says, "And of some have compassion, making a difference." Showing compassion to people you may not feel like showing compassion to can make a difference in their lives and bring them to repentance and salvation.

I pray, Father, You would help me to have a heart of compassion, sympathy, kindness, and friendliness toward others so that they would see You in me.

MY REFLECTION:

DAY 54
ADDRESSING GOD BY NAME

PSALM 55:16

"As for me, I will call upon God; and the LORD shall save me."

"As for me, I will cry out to, properly address by name and call upon the exceedingly great God; and the self-existent Lord will save, help, deliver, rescue, and preserve me, so I can get the victory." (NWI)

One of the interesting things I have discovered recently is the importance of addressing God by His name. You may wonder why that is; or maybe, like me, you'd never thought much about it.

God has been revealing to me in His Word, in several different locations, that it is important. When I thought about it, I finally had more understanding.

If I was in a crowd of people and someone just yelled, "Hey!" I may or may not know they were referring to me.

If someone called out to me, "Mrs. White!" I would know it was either someone that didn't know me well or a former student.

If someone called out to me, "Nancy!" I would know it was a person that knew me to a greater degree—possibly as a friend or family member.

Then again, if someone yelled out to me, "Mom!" I would know it was one of my sons—or "Nana!" for one of my grandchildren. Each of those names refers to a different part of me and affects how I respond to the person. How much more is this true for the God of the universe, the Creator of all that we know, our Healer, our Savior, Jesus, Lord, Holy Spirit, Deliverer, Comforter, Provider, Joy, Hope. Just as I like to be called by my name and would know how to respond to the person based on how they addressed me, so the Lord likes to be called by His name as well.

As we approach the Lord in prayer, let's remember who we are talking to based on our prayer need and address Him by that name.

Lord, I come to You thanking You for who You are. Thank You that You are my Savior, Healer, Peace, Provider, Comforter, Joy, Hope, Almighty, Strength, Light, Wisdom, Husband, Friend, and all I need.

MY REFLECTION:

_____

_____

_____

_____

_____

_____

_____

_____

_____

_____

_____

_____

_____

_____

_____

_____

_____

_____

_____

_____

_____

_____

DAY 55
DIVINE INFLUENCE ON THE HEART

EPHESIANS 2:8

"For by grace are ye saved through faith; and that
not of yourselves: it is the gift of God."

*"For by the divine influence upon your heart and its reflection in
your life are you saved, delivered, protected, preserved, healed,
and made whole through the channel of the act of your faith, your
assurance and reliance upon Christ; and that not of your own selves,
it is the sacrifice and gift of the Supreme divinity, God." (NWI)*

The amazing gift we receive by asking Jesus to be in our lives and relying on Him for everything comes about because God loves us so very much. Through Jesus's death and resurrection, He provided for us to be saved, delivered, protected, preserved, healed, and made whole. He is our peace that passes understanding when we are going through difficult times. It's not that we'll never ever have another problem; it's that, in and through our hard circumstances, He will be by our side, helping, leading, comforting, providing, encouraging, and showing His love for us.

We must remember that it is not anything we have done that was good enough, or even that we were able to have enough strength to push through and endure. It is solely by God's grace and mercy extended to us through the shedding of His Son's blood, death, and resurrection that we are able to obtain our salvation, which includes healing, deliverance, protection, provision, peace, and being made whole. God knew we wouldn't be able to obtain these things on our own, so He allowed His Son, Jesus, to go through everything for us so that, when we ask Him into our hearts, we will not only have eternal life with Him but have what we need on earth as well.

Lord, help me to realize that it's not through my own ability that I am able to make it through my difficult and sometimes dark days, but that it's through Your gift of Jesus living and abiding in me through faith. He provides all that I need.

MY REFLECTION:

DAY 56
PEACE

DEUTERONOMY 31:8c

"... fear not, neither be dismayed."

"Don't be frightened, or else be broken down." (NWI)

When we let fear grip our mind, spirit, or emotions, it causes us to be anxious, afraid, depressed, discouraged, confused, and even terrified about something that may or may not ever occur. It robs us of the moment. It breaks us down.

Rather than remembering the first part of the verse that Moses tells Joshua—which says the Lord would go before him, be with him, and not fail him or forsake him—we look at all the possible circumstances and problems, setting our eyes on the "what ifs," the "bad news," or very real problems. Even if there is a genuine concern, dwelling on it doesn't help. Our peace comes from the Lord. If we will turn our thoughts to the One who can do something about the situation, rest, and trust Him, He can give us strength, joy, peace, hope, and courage. That sounds like a great exchange to me! The problem may never go away, but by surrendering your fears and concerns to Him in prayer, it opens up the possibility. Even if things stay the same, I would much rather rest in His peace and joy than be fearful, anxious, confused, or panicked all the time.

Take note once again that we see this as a decision. Moses told Joshua not to be afraid or dismayed, but it was still Joshua's choice as to whether he would trust the Lord or continue to walk in fear and anxiety. Moses, God, and even the people of Israel repeatedly had to remind Joshua to "fear not, neither be dismayed." Why? I believe it is because it was a genuine issue that Joshua had to deal with, so he needed to be reminded to trust God.

Fear is something I have had to continuously get the victory over throughout the years. Just as God reminded Joshua, He gently reminded me over and over again not to be afraid but to trust Him. He is now reminding you to trust Him for your circumstance rather than being anxious, broken down, depressed, or fearful. His desire is to see us whole, blessed, and in peace.

Lord, help me to surrender my problems to You and trust You with them.

MY REFLECTION:

DAY 57
CHOOSING

EPHESIANS 4:31
"Let all bitterness, and wrath, and anger, and clamour, and
evil speaking, be put away from you, with all malice."

*"Let all things that have been left around and that have survived,
and your fierce passion and indignation, and anger, justifiable
abhorrence, and violent ire, and outcries of grief and crying, and
railing, especially against God, be lifted and sail away from you, with
all badness, naughtiness, wickedness, and maliciousness." (NWI)*

T he word "let" is a word that indicates a choice. We can choose to allow bitterness, wrath, anger, evil speaking, fierce passion, railing against God, wickedness, and everything else that brings us down as well—as others around us—to be put away from us, or we can allow those things to stay with us.

When someone does something against us, intentionally or not, it is easy to wallow in it, have a grudge against that person, talk about that situation, and stay angry. But as Christians, God has called us to a better way of living. Those intense emotions only bring us to a state of a possible heart attack or keep us trapped in unhealthy feelings. Unforgiveness really hurts us more than the person with whom we are angry. So we have a choice. We can forgive and walk in God's peace, or we can stay angry, lose relationships, and quite possibly cause ourselves to become ill.

In addition, take notice of the wording, "that have been left around and that have survived." This is a reminder to let go of the things in our past. Also, take notice of the wording in the NWI, "be lifted and sail away from you" further illustrates what we should do with past issues that we've allowed to linger in our lives. It reminds me of the demonstration of putting your problems into a balloon and letting them go. Quite literally, they are lifted away from you. We can do the same thing by lifting up our problems, past or present, to the Lord and giving them to Him, relinquishing all the rights and powers they held over us. He will take our burdens for us.

Lord, I pray that, instead of holding onto the things that people have done to me—which fills me with anger and bitterness—I would choose to forgive and walk in the freedom You have provided for me.

MY REFLECTION:

DAY 58
ENCOURAGING YOURSELF

1 SAMUEL 30:6

"And David was greatly distressed; for the people spake of stoning him, because the soul of all the people was grieved, every man for his sons and for his daughters: but David encouraged himself in the LORD his God."

"And David was vehemently, wholly, exceedingly vexed, distressed, and felt pressed; for the people spoke about stoning him, because the soul of all the people was bitter, rebellious and disobedient, every man for his sons and for his daughters: but David fastened himself to the Lord his God which helped, repaired, established, recovered, and made him valiant so that he could continue and withstand to do what he needed to do." (NWI)

King David, the man God called "a man after His own heart," was "exceedingly distressed" because his people were talking about stoning him. I love the fact that this verse clearly states that the people's rebellious heart caused David to be exceedingly distressed, because he has now become human, someone I can relate to—someone that shares my emotions. They had bitter and rebellious hearts and were taking their grief for their missing families out on David.

We do that too, don't we? We take our fears, worries, and concerns out on the ones in front of us by being angry with them instead of turning these problems over to the Lord. Through this experience, we can see why David had God's heart: he didn't stay gripped by fear; instead, he "encouraged himself in the Lord his God." In other words, he wasn't going to let go of God. Now his fear and distress are turned to strength, courage, and help. David has recovered, and he knows what to do.

At this point, David asks God whether he should pursue the Amalekites that had burned their city and taken their wives and children. The Lord tells him to do it. David inquired of God and asked something seemingly obvious; and yet he had the wisdom not to go into this battle without the Lord's presence. When we take our eyes off the looming problem in front of us and seek the Lord, He will give us wisdom, direction, strength, and courage. In this situation, God helped David and his men find and bring their families back home.

Had David remained distressed and not sought after God's wisdom, quite possibly his men would have stoned him, their families may not have been retrieved, and all David was able to accomplish as king would not have occurred. His simple act of seeking God in the midst of great turmoil, anguish, anger, and grief enabled him to bring back their families, fulfill his purpose, and realize God's faithfulness.

Lord, help me to be more like Your servant David in that, when he was terrified for his life, he gave that fear to You and asked for wisdom to know what to do.

MY REFLECTION:

DAY 59
NOT ALONE

HEBREWS 2:18

"For in that he himself hath suffered being tempted,
he is able to succour them that are tempted."

*"For in that He Himself has experienced the feeling of the pain
of being scrutinized, disciplined, examined, tried, proven, and
tested, it enables Him to have the ability and the power for
Him to help, aid, and relieve those that are being scrutinized,
disciplined, examined, tried, proven, and tested." (NWI)*

When we are going through tough times, it sometimes feels like we are very alone. The devil would like nothing better than for us to feel like no one cares, no one else is going to understand, no one else will "get it," or that we are the only ones.

This verse clarifies the truth that we are definitely not alone. Even if there is not another person on earth that has experienced what you are experiencing (which, according to the Bible, is not the case), there is always One who has been through what you are going through and understands. Jesus understands everything we are dealing with because He has personally experienced it Himself. Therefore, when we go to Him in prayer, we can be assured that there is Someone who cares and will help us through our problems as we lean on His understanding and not our own.

Whether the problem is physical, emotional, financial, mental, relational, or in any other area of life, God understands and will be there for you. We don't have to be in fear, we don't have to worry, and we don't have to be depressed. As we lean into Him, He will make a way where there seems to be no way. The outcome may not be what we want, but He will not leave us. He will provide, He will heal, He will deliver, He will save, because He is the Great I Am! He is everything we need!

Father, as I come to You, I lift up my needs according to Your Word, believing that You have my best interest in mind and will perform Your Word according to Your riches in glory by Christ Jesus. I trust You for all of my needs to be met, knowing that You understand and will help me through everything I am going through.

MY REFLECTION:

DAY 60
REFUGE

PSALM 9:9

"The Lord also will be a refuge for the oppressed, a refuge in times of trouble."

*"The Lord will be a refuge, defense, and high fort for those
who are crushed, injured, afflicted or oppressed, a defense,
high tower and refuge in long seasons of continual tightness,
adversity, anguish, affliction, distress, and trouble." (NWI)*

We have all had those seasons of life when it seems like one thing after another is happening around us or to us. Everywhere you turn, something is breaking, difficulties arise, people are becoming ill or dying, problems occur at work, money is tight, and so on.

If we choose to turn these problems, afflictions, hurts, struggles and concerns over to the Lord, He will be a high tower and refuge for us. What does that mean? If you are in a battle, and you stay in the midst of it for a long period of time, besides the fact that you could be injured, you will also become weary and emotionally drained. But if you can get to a high tower, it will at least temporarily give you a place to rest, have your wounds tended to, be nourished, be refreshed, and help you be ready to deal with the enemy again. It also enables you to see the whole battle from a new perspective.

When we are in those long, continual seasons of adversity, distress, or trouble, if we will go to the Lord and seek Him, He will be that "high tower," that refuge, for us.

Thank You, Lord, for being my place of refuge when I am in trouble. Thank You for being my Healer, Rescuer, and Defender when I am going through a difficult time. Help me to come to You in times of need rather than trying to fight and tackle the problem on my own.

MY REFLECTION:

DAY 61
BE KIND

EPHESIANS 4:32

"And be ye kind one to another, tenderhearted, forgiving one another, even as God for Christ's sake hath forgiven you."

"And you be useful in your manner and morals, be better, kind, and gracious to each other, sympathetic, compassionate, and tenderhearted, freely and frankly giving forgiveness that pardons, rescues, and delivers yourself as well as them, even as God our Supreme Divinity for Jesus the Messiah's giving of Himself wholly to being kind, pardoning, rescuing, delivering, and freely giving forgiveness to you." (NWI)

This used to be a favorite Bible verse of mine—I would quote it to my two sons as they grew up, so much so that it became a standard joke. They would say, "Be ye kind" to me with much sarcasm. But honestly, it is a quote we should all remember every day of our lives.

It seems there is always someone being murdered, people who are offended and rude, families breaking apart, stealing, cheating, lies—you name it. There is always something occurring that can easily rile us up and cause us to stay that way.

But God's Word tells us, through the apostle Paul, that we should be kind, sympathetic, compassionate, tenderhearted, and forgiving each other, just like Jesus did with and for us. The verb "be" is a choice, as in "to be or not to be" from Shakespeare. We can choose to use good morals and manners, or we can choose to be rude and unkind, holding a grudge. If we choose the latter, we may not understand that the person we see as our immediate enemy may actually be going through a rough time and, unfortunately, taking it out on us. We can choose to try to understand that we all have difficult times and occasions when we don't act our best. This creates an attitude more suited to forgiving the person.

I am so very thankful for my family, friends, and even strangers that have forgiven me of my bad attitudes. It doesn't mean you have to like what the person did. It just says we are to show kindness, tenderheartedness, sympathy, and compassion, like Jesus did to and for us.

The benefit isn't just for the person that offended us, either. The Bible says if we forgive others, our prayers will be answered and God will forgive us of our sins. I don't know about you, but those are two big motivators for me.

Lord, help me to live by Your example and show others the same love, compassion, grace, kindness, and forgiveness that You have so abundantly shown me.

MY REFLECTION:

DAY 62
PROVIDER

PSALM 18:39a

"For thou hast girded me with strength unto the battle. . . ."

"For you have bound, compassed about, and girded me with an army of resources, wealth, virtue, strength, ability, training, might, power, riches, substance, and worth for the war, battle and fight." (NWI)

L ife hands us many "curveballs," doesn't it? Everything is going as planned, things are good, and them, *wham*! Something happens that you never expected.

The possibilities are endless: your spouse has an affair, your daughter becomes pregnant while still in high school, you or a loved one is diagnosed with cancer or a rare disease, you have a serious car accident, a friend commits suicide, your company goes under, your house burns down, a tree falls on your house, a child has an addiction to drugs or alcohol, your job transfers you to a new state, a loved one dies, and on and on goes the list. Those, and so many other scenarios, can debilitate us, put us into fear, cause depression, and defeat us if we keep our eyes on them.

Instead, when we are in the midst of a battle, we can turn to the Lord for our help. When we do, He will provide the resources we need to get through the circumstances. When we feel weak, He gives strength; when we are financially lacking, He provides; when we don't know what to do, He gives wisdom and direction; when we are fearful, He brings peace. He has an "army of resources" at His disposal if we will but turn our distresses over to Him.

Lord, help me put my problems into Your hands rather than trying to carry them myself, because You have everything it takes to handle it all.

MY REFLECTION:

DAY 63
REST

EXODUS 34:21

"Six days you will work, but on the seventh day you will
rest, in earing time and in harvest you will rest."

Has God ever showed you something that brought about one of those "aha" moments? That's what happened to me when the Lord revealed one of His truths in Exodus 34:21

The word "earing" means "ploughing," and "harvest" means "to reap the crop." Of course, we all know God created everything in six days and rested on the seventh, the Sabbath, and that He wants us to do likewise. In Exodus 31:13, we can find out that we are to keep His Sabbath because "it is a sign between me and you throughout your generations; that you know that I am the Lord that does sanctify you." "It is holy unto you" and "holy to the Lord" (Exodus 31:14), "It is a perpetual covenant" (Exodus 31:16), and a "sign between me and the children of Israel forever" (Exodus 31:17). "On the seventh day he rested and was refreshed" (Exodus 31:17).

God wants us to rest even in our busiest times, when it is crucial that we work. In the agricultural society of that time (as well today), earing and harvest were time-sensitive. You had to get things done—if you didn't, it could cost you food and money: provision for your family and livestock. But God said, "Rest!" In today's society, everyone is so busy with work, deadlines, family, ballgames, lessons, school, house and yard work . . . it seems like there's no time to rest, but God still wants us to do it. Just as God provided manna for the people to eat, even providing more the day before the Sabbath so they wouldn't have to work to go out and gather it, God will provide before the Sabbath all that needs to be done, if we'll only honor it.

By resting on the Sabbath, we are trusting God and exercising our faith. If we'll obey His Word and keep His covenant of the Sabbath, He'll take care and provide for us. It's resting in Him and allowing God to do for us as only He can. Sure, keeping the Sabbath gives our physical bodies rest, but the bigger picture is that we have to extend our faith to believe that all the work we need to do will still get accomplished while we rest.

In Hebrew, the word *Sabbath* in Exodus means "intermission." In the theater, intermission is when the sets are changed or rearranged, the actors take a quick break to be refreshed and get ready for the next scene, and those in the audience have time to use the restroom, talk to each other, stretch their legs, and get some refreshments. Do you see that, when we take an "intermission" by resting on the Sabbath, God is able to get a lot done to be ready for the next scene for us? I love it!

In Hebrews 3 and 4, Paul describes how we enter into rest by belief. Hebrews 4:3 says, "For we which have believed do enter into rest, as he said, As I have sworn in my wrath, if they shall enter into my rest: although the works were finished from the foundation of the world." Hebrews 4:10 continues, "For he that is entered into his rest, he also hath ceased from his own works, as God did from His." This is a decision to cease from doing what I want or think needs to be done and to have faith that God knows best.

Hebrews 3:18 (NKJV) says, "And to whom did He swear that they would not enter His rest, but to those who did not obey?" The word *rest* in the Greek means, "abide, to settle down, cease, give rest (rain)." I love this! If we have faith that the Lord can do what we can't, and exercise that faith by ceasing from our works and refraining from trying to do it all in our own strength and ability, He can actually get more done than we can. I have no idea how He does it, but I can absolutely testify that this principle is 100% true!

It boils down to resting, trusting, and having faith in His ability. Instead of stressing about all that needs done and not having enough time to do it all, why not take God at His Word and honor His Sabbath? The Bible says God was refreshed when He rested on the seventh day. Honoring the Sabbath brings rest and refreshment for our mind, body and spirit to be able to do what we need to do for the next six days.

Father, help me honor Your Word and Your Sabbath.
Forgive me, Lord, for not being obedient to You in this
covenant. Help me, Lord, to have faith—to trust You.

MY REFLECTION:

_____

_____

_____

_____

_____

_____

_____

DAY 64
NEEDING THE LORD

PSALM 119:81

"My soul fainteth for thy salvation: but I hope in thy word."

"My mind, body, breath, soul, and will fails for Your deliverance, help, safety, salvation, and victory: but I will be patient, have hope and wait on Your advice, answer, power, promise, provision, purpose, and word." (NWI)

Everything that is of us—our natural ability, strength, and courage—will fail to achieve what only God can do in our lives. But if we wait on the Lord to perform His Word in us and in our situations, He will deliver us, save us, protect us, and tell us what we need to do. He will give us the answers we are seeking. He will give us strength and ability. He will fulfill His Word. He will provide and show us what our purpose is. Our plans can't bring us peace, faith, hope and joy, but when we patiently decide to trust God, He will provide the answers we are seeking.

We have somehow decided that we are better able to get things done than the One who created everything, the One who is all-powerful and all-knowing, the One who loves us and has our best interest at hand, the One who has already won the victory for us to be saved, healed, delivered, and helped. King David made the decision to trust patiently and have hope that God would lead and direct him, providing everything he needed. If the king of Israel, God's beloved son that had a heart after God, needed the Lord to give him wisdom, lead him, strengthen him, provide for him, show him his purpose, and help him, why wouldn't we need Him, as well? The answer is, we do need the Lord. David recognized his need for God; he knew that, without the Lord, he would fail. We need to make that same decision.

Father, I submit myself to You. I know You can bring about good in and through me if I will trust You. Help me to be dependent on You instead of myself. Lord, I will wait patiently for and have hope in Your advice, promises, provision, and salvation. As David did, I will have hope in Your Word and Your promises for me.

MY REFLECTION:

DAY 65
ATTRIBUTES OF GOD

JEREMIAH 31:34

"And they shall teach no more every man his neighbor, and every man his brother, saying, Know the Lord: for they shall all know me, from the least of them unto the greatest of them, saith the Lord: for I will forgive their iniquity, and I will remember their sin no more."

It seems everywhere you turn lately, something is going on that can bring fear, anxiety, stress, turmoil, discouragement, sadness, frustration, depression, etc. It could stem from financial problems, physical problems, death, marital issues, difficult children, a pandemic, politics, racial tension, and the list goes on and on. So much that it can be overwhelming. BUT GOD....

Instead of focusing on all of the problems, difficulties, hurts, injustices, and concerns, let's keep our eyes on the ONLY ONE WHO can actually do something about the issues. IF we can keep our eyes on Jesus rather that the storms that seem like tornadoes, hurricanes and whirlwinds in our lives, we can instead receive His peace that passes understanding, joy, hope, faith, His wisdom and understanding, and encouragement. As much as we want the problems to go away, there's always going to be something that can draw our eyes off of Him and to the gigantic issues that are before us. So, it basically boils down to the fact, that instead of worrying, being fearful, wanting to quit, etc. we should look to and trust the Lord that He has it all under control. It may not work out the way we wanted it to, or look like we think it should look, but if our eyes, heart and thoughts are focused on the Lord, we can know that "all things work together for good to them that love God. . . ." (Romans 8:28a). Maybe if we take our hands off of the situation to try to control it to be the way we think it should be and trust the One Who has our best interest in mind to take care of it, maybe, just maybe, we can have peace knowing that it's going to be okay.

Let's remember some of God's attributes, so that we can be reminded of Who HE IS:

- Faithful - 1 Corinthians 1:9
- Wiser that man - 1 Corinthians 1:25
- Merciful - Psalm 116:5
- With us - Isaiah 8:10
- Truth - Deuteronomy 32:4; Psalm 31:5
- Greater than our heart - I John 3:20
- Love - 1 John 4:8,16
- Your refuge - Deuteronomy 33:27
- My strength and power - II Samuel 22:33
- My helper - Psalm 54:4
- My defense - Zechariah 9:15
- My salvation - Isaiah 12:2
- Almighty - Genesis 17:1
- My husband - Hosea 2:16
- Patience - Romans 15:5
- My consolation - Romans 15:5
- Peace - Romans 15:13
- My provider - Genesis 22:8
- Love - 2 Corinthians 13:11
- All grace - 1 Peter 6:10
- King of Kings - I Timothy 6:5
- My Rock - 1 Corinthians 10:4
- Healer - Psalms 103:3
- Comforter - 2 Corinthians 1:3
- Deliverer - Psalm 91:3,15
- Forgiver - Luke 23:24
- With us - Isaiah 8:10
- Greater than our heart - I John 3:20

I think that about covers every need we might possibly have! May you be blessed today and rest in His arms.

Father, help me to trust You to take care of what is bringing me down, so that I will be able to be all that You have for me to be and do.

MY REFLECTION:

_____

_____

_____

_____

_____

_____

_____

_____

_____

_____

_____

DAY 66
PRIDE

HOSEA 8:3

"Israel hath cast off the thing that is good: the enemy shall pursue him."

At first glance, I didn't really see much in this scripture; but as I began to dwell on it, the Lord opened my eyes to some truths I hadn't noticed. The first thing that caught my attention was the statement, "Israel has cast off." Israel (we) made a choice to cast off/throw away/get rid of "the thing that is good." When we throw away the things God has given us for our good—when we don't regard His Word, when we decide we can do it all rather than turning it over to the Lord—we are opening the door to be ensnared and entangled by the enemy.

Basically, it all boils down to one word: *pride.* Pride is thinking we can do things without God's help or leading. We might be able to "pull it off" for a while, thinking that, because of our pride, it's all under control. But unfortunately, we get a false sense of accomplishment. Proverbs 16:18 says that "pride goeth before destruction." Proverbs 29:23 says, ". . . a man's pride shall bring him low." Obadiah 3 (ESV) says, "The pride of your heart has deceived you." Pride is literally deceiving and gives us a wrong perception of our own ability and importance.

Proverbs 8:13 says, "The fear of the Lord is to hate evil: pride, and arrogancy." Instead of thinking "we can do all things," we need to remember the rest of the verse: "through Christ who strengthens me" (Philippians 4:13, NKJV). It's only with the help of Jesus that we are able to "do all things."

It's only when we surrender our lives, our problems, our hurts, our family, our marriage, our children, our job, our illnesses, and our financial problems, and let God work on them for us, that we will see change. He is able to do "exceedingly abundantly above all that we ask or think, according to the power that worketh in us" (Ephesians 3:20). We are limited in our own strength and ability, but He's not limited.

I choose not to cast off the thing that is good. I choose God's way. I choose to believe His Word and submit to His authority, His strength, His ability, and I choose to walk in His faith and hope.

Thank You, Lord, for Your Word that gives light and instructions even in places we least expect. Father, I choose to surrender my pride to You, and I submit to trusting You for everything in my life.

MY REFLECTION:

DAY 67
DECEIVED

OBADIAH 3a

"The pride of your heart has deceived you." (NKJV)

So often, we try to "fix things" in our lives or situations based on our ability, strength, wisdom, understanding, connections, or position, with the misunderstanding that we can do whatever comes our way. There may be times when it appears that this is true in our lives, when in actuality, those moments stem from a root of pride. According to this verse, pride is deceiving me to think I am the one that is able to take care of myself or my family.

There will come a time when it seems as if nothing is going smoothly. Try as I might, the problems will become bigger than I am able to manage by myself. At some point, the reality hits me that it's more than my ability and strength, and I don't know what to do except pray! Well, hello! That is what God has been trying to get me to see all along. The problems, circumstances, and situations are all more than I can handle by myself.

Prayer should be my first response rather than my last response. When I am praying, I am surrendering myself and my problems to the Lord to take care of them. It's not that God wants us to go through these hard times, but it's that through the difficult times we come to the realization that we're not God. He is all-powerful, all-knowing, all-understanding. He is able, and nothing is too difficult for Him. But just like Jesus had to surrender Himself to the Father and suffer on the cross in order to gain the victory over sin, sickness, death, and everything else for us, we must sometimes go through what feels like agony and suffering for God to bring about our victory—or that of a loved one. Jesus had to totally rely on His Father's promise, just like we have to totally rely on our Heavenly Father's promises to us in His Word. It's not our ability, but His!

James 4:10 declares: "Humble yourselves in the sight of the Lord, and He shall lift you up." Humility is the opposite of pride. God wants us to be humble before Him so that He can do exploits on our behalf. Our pride limits us because we are limited in what we can do in and of ourselves. In Proverbs 22:4 we learn that it's "By humility and the fear of the Lord are riches, and honor, and life."

One of my favorite verses is Matthew 6:33: "But seek ye first the kingdom of God, and His righteousness; and all these things shall be added unto you." God sees our needs, knows how to take care of us, and desires to do so; but we must look to Him for our answers. As we do, He will "supply all of your need according to His riches in glory by Christ Jesus" (Philippians 4:19).

Father, forgive me for not seeking You first for solutions to my problems, needs, and situations. Help me always to look to You for my answers rather than thinking I can do it all by myself. I am limited, but You are not. I humble myself before You, thankful that You are able to take care of my requests.

MY REFLECTION:

DAY 68
STORMS OF LIFE

LUKE 8:23

"But as they sailed he fell asleep: and there came down a storm of wind on the lake; and they were filled with water, and were in jeopardy."

"But as they sailed he fell asleep: and there came down a storm of wind, a whirlwind on the lake; and the boat was completely filled with water, and they were in danger, jeopardy, undergoing peril." (NWI)

This familiar narrative is found in three of the gospels. We see it in Matthew 8:23-27, Mark 4:35-41, and Luke 8:22-25. Mark's account goes into more detail than the others, whereby we learn that Jesus had just finished sharing many parables to the multitudes of people along the seashore. He then further explained them to the twelve disciples, which took all day until the evening. After sending away the multitudes, the disciples took him into the ship, but there were other, smaller ships as well. The wind was so great that it caused the ship to be full of water.

Jesus was sleeping on a pillow in the back of the ship. When things got really bad, they woke Him up and said, "Master, don't You care that we are about to die?" At that point, Jesus got up, rebuked the wind, told the sea, "Peace, be still," and both did what they were told to do. There was great calm. He then asked the disciples why they were so afraid—why they didn't have any faith.

I began wondering about the storms that rage in our lives—the tempests that are loud, surging, dangerous, and coming from every direction. I was challenged to be like Jesus rather than the disciples. He spoke, charged, and forbid the waves to be so loud and forceful—they had reached a point where the storm was all the disciples could hear or feel. Jesus literally muted and muzzled the storm so that it could no longer be a threat, and there was tranquility, peace and calm.

What storms might be raging in our lives? Among many, there might be financial crisis, marital problems, the loss of a loved one, negative medical news, addictions, work- or family-related issues, depression, and several others. These can be powerful storms with damaging winds that could literally destroy us, if left to their own devices. Jesus showed the disciples how to deal with tempests that can knock us off our feet.

Firstly, He had already told the disciples, "Let us go over unto the other side of the lake." He had given them directions: what they were going to do and where they were going. But along the way, things got rough, and the disciples succumbed to their fears. That isn't to say that it wasn't terrifying, but Jesus said they were going to go to the other side, and then He fell asleep. They could have chosen to go where He was and trust what He had just told them. They could have rested in His promise. Likewise, if God gives us a word, we need to hold onto what He has given us rather than becoming fearful of the commotion around us.

Secondly, when they roused Jesus, notice that He didn't deny the storm was real. He did, however, rebuke them for being afraid of it rather than resting in what He had told them. Jesus addressed the issues at hand. On the other hand, the disciples, instead of resting and trusting in the Word He had given them before the storm hit, were overcome with the power and strength of the storm and the understanding of what *could* happen. The storm was, after all, *real*! Jesus didn't ignore it, but He did forbid it from doing what it *could* do. He spoke directly to the tumultuous winds and surging waters. The disciples were astonished that the elements obeyed Him, and at the tranquility and peace that resulted.

When it was all over, "they arrived at the country of the Gadarenes which is over against Galilee" (Luke 8:26). In other words, they made it to their destination, just as Jesus had told them. The storm could have destroyed the boat, injuring or even killing the people onboard. Instead, they reached their destination safely.

So then, it appears there are three options we can choose in the midst of storms:

1) Do absolutely nothing and see what happens.
2) Be totally fearful and succumb to the storm's destruction.
3) Go to Jesus in the midst of the storm—and our fear—and seek His help. He has power over everything, including storms, and they must obey Him. Since we, as believers, have the same power and authority as Jesus, we also can rebuke the storms of life and they must obey us, as well.

One thing that isn't mentioned—but that is certainly a very real factor in this story—is if there was any damage done. There could have been broken boards, torn sails, or other repercussions of the storm. People on the ship could have sustained bumps and bruises. Sometimes, we are affected by the storms we must go through. They may even leave scars; but we can still have the ultimate victory of making it through to the destination the Lord purposed us to reach.

Notice that, when Jesus rebuked the wind and raging waters, the disciples were in awe and reverence of Jesus. Likewise, when others see us using the gifts and authority provided by Jesus to be victorious over dire situations in our lives, it will cause others to take notice and draw them to Jesus.

Lord, help me to rest and trust in You when I am going through storms. Help me to quickly go to You in the midst of the storm—and my fears—to seek Your help. Guide me in using the power and authority You have provided to "mute, muzzle, and quiet" the storm. Help me bring peace, calm, and tranquility into the situation and my life.

MY REFLECTION:

DAY 69
GUIDING LIGHT

PSALM 32:8

"I will instruct thee and teach thee in the way which
thou shalt go: I will guide thee with mine eye."

*"I will make you to understand and have wisdom and I will point out to teach
you in the way and manner in which you should go, walk, depart, follow, grow,
prosper, or pursue: I will advise and guide you with my presence." (NWI)*

A s we spend time seeking God, He will honor His Word to help us. If we need direction and understanding about what we should do in a situation, He will give it to us. If we need wisdom to know how to do something, He'll provide it. He will lead and guide us along the path we are to take.

We must be able to distinguish His voice from that of the world's. The way to do this is by being in His presence and in His Word. God actually desires to be with us—to be intimate with us. He wants us to be in His presence so that we discern when He is guiding us. The way we recognize individuals' voices is by listening to them and being with them. The same holds true with the Lord. The way we learn to recognize His voice is by being with Him in worship, prayer and reading His Word.

Another way to determine if what we are hearing is from the Lord is to know whether it goes along with God's Word. But in order to do that, we must spend time in the Bible. The Bible is filled with His wisdom, directions, understanding and encouragement. The more time we spend in God's Word, the more we will recognize His voice when He speaks to us.

Father, thank You for Your Word that helps me when I need wisdom,
direction, and understanding for what I am going through.

MY REFLECTION:

DAY 70
PRAYING IN FAITH

MATTHEW 7:3

"And why do you look at the speck in your brother's eye, but
do not consider the plank in your own eye?" (NKJV)

I love how God works! As I was praying for various family members and friends, I felt like the Lord was using this scripture to reveal something to me. I didn't realize my prayers were derogatory towards anyone, but God was trying to show me that I had been praying incorrectly. After swallowing my pride, I asked Him what I was doing wrong, and to please forgive me.

Much to my surprise, the Lord quickly gave me an answer by letting me know what I had been doing wrong. He showed me that my prayers came from fear rather than trust and faith. Well, talk about being caught off-guard! I had not even realized I was doing that. But as I thought everything over, and evaluated my prayer life objectively, I understood what the Lord was so graciously allowing me to know.

Most of the time I had been praying—especially if there was an emergency, or a loved one going through difficulties—I was quoting and declaring scriptures of God's promises for the subject of my prayers. . . . which seems right, doesn't it? But rather than declaring God's promises for the individual out of faith, my declarations had been brought about by fear. As I grabbed hold of what God was trying to show me, I learned how to pray differently.

Rather than praying because I'm afraid of what could happen, I began praying more out of my trust and confidence of what God can and will do, leaving the problems with Him, and exercising my faith in His ability to do the impossible. I'm seeing His promises differently as I declare them, because they are now truths I can rely on rather than things I am grasping for in desperation.

I don't know if anyone else is doing the same thing I did; but just in case, I want to challenge you like God challenged me. Stop praying from a place of fear and start praying from a place of faith and victory, trusting Him!

Dear Lord, I lift up my fears to You as I lift up my needs. Help me to see with Your eyes, understand with Your wisdom, and trust You. As I give You my prayer concerns, I thank You that I can pray out of Your victory, because You have already shown Yourself faithful in my life. I know You will make a way where there seems to be no way. Your Word is truth, and I can depend on You.

MY REFLECTION:

_____

_____

_____

_____

_____

_____

_____

_____

_____

_____

_____

_____

_____

_____

_____

_____

_____

_____

_____

_____

_____

_____

DAY 71

HANGING OUT

PSALM 34:4

"I sought the Lord, and he heard me, and delivered
me from all my fears." (NKJV)

*"I frequented with the Lord and asked Him questions to search
out and seek inquisition, and He paid attention to me and He
responded to me by bearing witness with song, testimony, and
giving account, and rescued me so that I could escape from all
my places of fear and terrors where I tend to dwell." (NWI)*

G od loves it when we "hang out" with Him, just like parents love to be with their children. He loves to help us with our problems.

Reading this verse reminds me of a child that has a problem that they need to talk to their parents about. The parents listen to the concern and respond in ways that encourage the child, bring clarity, and make them feel better. The parents are able to take away the fear and even the terrors the child might have about the situation. This is what the Lord does for us as well.

When we come to Him, lay out our problems before Him and ask Him questions about what to do or how to handle things, He reminds us of His Word, meaningful songs, or testimonies of others that have been through the same situation and who have gained the victory. When we spend this crucial time with the Lord, we are encouraged, we have hope, and we no longer worry about the problem because we have His peace.

> Father, help me to come to You with my questions and concerns
> so that You can help me and lead me to the answer.

MY REFLECTION:

DAY 72
ESCAPE

1 CORINTHIANS 10:13

"There hath no temptation taken you but such as is common to man: but God is faithful, who will not suffer you to be tempted above that ye are able; but will with the temptation also make a way to escape, that ye may be able to bear it."

"There has no experience of evil, or adversity come on you but such as is common to mankind: but God is trustworthy, faithful, and true and will not leave you alone to be tested, enticed, proven, scrutinized or tried beyond or more than you are able , have the power and might, or can do; but will with the provocation, adversity, experience of evil or proof by experiment of good, also provide, purpose, and make a way to escape, that you may be of power and it may be possible to undergo the hardship, endure from underneath it and bear it." (NWI)

God's Word never says we won't have difficulties, but we can repeatedly see examples of the above scripture revealed. We see it in the story of Daniel in the lion's den, Peter in prison, Jonah in the belly of the great fish, and Moses and the children of Israel crossing the Red Sea on dry land, to list a few examples. The Lord is with us.

Hebrews 13:5b says He "never leaves us nor forsakes us". Even though we may be going through tough times that seem overwhelming, we must remember that our loving, Heavenly Father is right there with us to help us make it through to victory. As we continuously seek Him, we can be sure that He will strengthen us, send us help, and encourage us through His Word. In the Bible, we can read that God caused the lions to not harm Daniel when he was put in the lion's den by King Darius (Daniel 6:16-22);an angel broke the chains off of Peter when he was imprisoned by Herod (Acts 12:1-7); a section of the Red Sea was dried up so that the Israelites were able to walk on dry land, and then the same wall of water came crashing down and drowned their enemy (Exodus

14:19-29); Jesus fed 5,000 plus people with five loaves of bread and two fish and had 12 baskets full of left overs (Matthew 14:15-20); and the examples can go on and on. In other words, God can do the impossible on our behalf if we will trust Him.

Our hope shouldn't be in what *we* can do, but in what God is able to do as we keep our eyes on Him. He is a "way-maker" where there doesn't seem to be a way. We need to realize that sometimes, the answer isn't going to come immediately, and sometimes it's different than the answer we expected. But if we keep our eyes on the Answer, He will come through. The great part is that, in the midst of it all, God can and does provide the "peace of God, which passeth all understanding" (Philippians 4:7) that enables us to stay strong and believe Him to do what only He can do.

Help me, Lord, to keep my eyes on You in the midst of trials, temptations, and when I'm being enticed, that I would see You holding my hand and walking beside me.

MY REFLECTION:

_____

_____

_____

_____

_____

_____

_____

_____

_____

_____

_____

_____

_____

_____

_____

_____

_____

_____

DAY 73
NOT FORGOTTEN

PSALM 34:7

"The angel of the LORD encampeth round about
them that fear him, and delivereth him."

*"The angel of the Lord, a teacher, prophet, or priest stays around
and dwells with them that revere the Lord, strengthens him,
gets him ready, prepares, and arms him to fight." (NWI)*

Have you noticed that, when you are going through a difficult time, the Lord provides people in your life to encourage you, help you, prepare you and show you what to do in difficult circumstances?

There are even supernatural times when He will send an angel to fight on your behalf. I have personally witnessed and experienced these things happen a number of times. It is such a blessing to know that we are never alone as long as we are seeking Him. God sees what we are dealing with and provides what or who we need to help us to be overcomers.

It might be that your pastor will preach on something at church that is exactly what you needed to hear. Perhaps a friend will call you and share something that ministers to you. People will provide just what you need, usually unknowingly, at just the right time. You will be assured that God sees you and that He hasn't forgotten about you. Remember, He knows your name, how many hairs you have on your head, and hears your cries.

When He does send someone to help you, it shows that you are not forgotten. I have had God even send help through some pretty unlikely places and circumstances; but since God is not limited, He is able to use whatever is needed. I had a friend who was encouraged during a difficult time she was going through with her daughter by reading a bulletin board along the side of a road. It literally had the exact thing she had been praying about written on it. We need to remember that the Lord is always with us and is always willing to help us, deliver us, provide for us, and show us His love. We just need to rest and trust Him.

Lord, I pray I would be reminded of the many ways in which you help me during difficult times. I pray You would open my eyes to see what You are providing for me, so that I can thank You and rest in Your love for me.

MY REFLECTION:

_____

_____

_____

_____

_____

_____

_____

_____

_____

_____

_____

_____

_____

_____

_____

_____

_____

_____

_____

_____

_____

DAY 74

NEGLECT NOT THE GIFT

I TIMOTHY 4:1, 3-5, 14-16

"Now the Spirit speaketh expressly, that in the latter times some shall depart from the faith, giving heed to seducing spirits, and doctrines of devils . . . Forbidding to marry, and commanding to abstain from meats, which God hath created to be received with thanksgiving of them which believe and know the truth. For every creature of God is good, and nothing to be refused, if it be received with thanksgiving: for it is sanctified by the word of God and prayer . . . Neglect not the gift that is in thee, which was given thee by prophecy, with the laying on of the hands of the presbytery. Meditate upon these things; give thyself wholly to them; that thy profiting may appear to all. Take heed unto thyself, and unto the doctrine; continue in them: for in doing this thou shalt both save thyself, and them that hear thee."

Without question, the first verses address the times we are living in completely. But the part that was convicting to me personally was verses 14-16. Because of circumstances, I had put on hold "the gift that is in me," and would even go so far as to say that I almost gave it up and quit out of frustration, discouragement, and doubt.

As a senior woman, I wondered how God could even use me. It all seemed senseless and futile to pursue what God put in my heart so long ago. I wasn't able to rest, though, because it was still burning in me and was lit in my spirit. God had never "opened the door" as I imagined—whether it was my fault, my misunderstanding, or just not God's timing, I don't know. I literally went out on two different occasions and bought wardrobes to wear for "whenever it happened" so that I would be ready for Him to use me. But nothing happened like I had anticipated.

What I do know is that, every time I read this passage, I am reminded of what I thought God spoke to me more than 45 years ago. I am reminded of the words of prophecy, given an endless number of times, that encouraged me along this journey—including in the recent past. So, yet again, I am giving back to the Lord what I felt He spoke to me to do. Whatever that looks like. I asked God's forgiveness for "holding on" to the things I felt He spoke to me about myself and my family, when it appears I misunderstood what He was telling me. I asked for God's help in releasing it all to Him and being content with what He was going to do in my life, knowing that He had it under control.

After I surrendered my preconceived ideas and allowed Him to lead and guide me, I once again found purpose and joy. Instead of waiting for that "big thing" to happen, I was doing the many things He put in front of me. I began sending out scriptures via text message to friends and family going through difficult times. I started doing what I could at church, like being a greeter, going twenty minutes early to church to do preservice intercessory prayer, being on the prayer team, and reaching out to those in need. I found out that the "big thing" I had been reaching for all of my adult life was right in front of me all of the time. My frustration ended, my joy returned, and I am so excited to watch God work.

Are you like me? Have you been waiting for that "big thing" you imagined God wanting you to do? Maybe that "big thing" is being like Jesus washing His disciples' feet. Maybe we are missing a lot of God's purposes for our lives because we aren't looking for the things He is pointing us to, but rather trying to be "someone important." I challenge you to surrender yourself, to be ready to do the everyday caring work for those the Lord puts in your path—to be ready to help those in need.

This topic reminds me of Mother Teresa. She did the most mundane of chores in the humblest of surroundings, and yet she is one of the most famous people in modern times. Let's keep our eyes open to those God is putting in our path, so we will see how to minister to them. Then, we can watch as God transforms their lives.

> Lord, I pray that I, as well my family, would be obedient to Your calling and not quit. I pray that I would see with Your eyes and not fixate on the "impossibility" of the situation. Help me to operate in Your will, Your calling, Your vision, and Your power and anointing. Help me to "do what Jesus did" and serve others.

MY REFLECTION:

DAY 75
GOD OF WONDERS

PSALM 77:14

"Thou art the God that doest wonders: thou hast
declared thy strength among the people."

*"You are the Almighty, powerful, strong God that makes, accomplishes, and
performs miracles and marvelous things: You have known, declared, and
shown Your might and strength to prevail among Your people." (NWI)*

I love this Psalm because it boldly declares who God is. If we can remember these attributes of His, we won't need to worry or fret about anything. He is: Almighty, powerful, and strong—meaning nothing is too difficult for Him. Then, the psalmist declares that God performs miracles, which are the things too high for us to even comprehend. They are things that can only happen miraculously, because they are impossible to accomplish any other way.

Finally, the verse states that God knows what we're dealing with in life. How comforting! He is able. He is willing. He performs miracles and accomplishes marvelous things. He has declared it in His Word. He is powerful. Glory to His Name!

> Lord, may I always remember and never doubt
> who You are and what You can do.

MY REFLECTION:

DAY 76

FOLLOWING GOD'S LEAD

PSALM 86:11

"Teach me thy way, O Lᴏʀᴅ; I will walk in thy truth;
unite my heart to fear thy name."

*"Point out to me with Your finger, direct, instruct, and inform me in
Your road that I am to trod, O Lord; I will continually go forward, grow
and walk in Your stability and faithfulness; join my heart, courage,
mind and understanding to become one with You to revere Your
individuality, honor, authority, character, and name." (NWI)*

Truly, this is my heart's cry—and I pray that it is the heart of every believer in Jesus. My desire is that God and I would have such an intimate relationship that I would be able to recognize His finger, so that when He is pointing it to give me direction, instruction, or information, I would know that it is Him leading me.

My next prayer is that I would continue to go forward, grow and walk in His stability and faith, not living in my past with fears, insecurities, hurts, weaknesses, uncertainties, or doubts.

My third prayer is that my heart, mind, courage, understanding, and every part of me would be one with Him, aligned with His authority, and that I would recognize God's individuality, name and character. In other words, I pray for the realization that I am operating in His wisdom, power, understanding, knowledge, strength, peace, and faith. I desire to give Him the praise and the glory. In myself, I am nothing; but with Him, "I can do all things through Christ which strengtheneth me" (Philippians 4:13)

Father, I pray that I would seek You first and lean on You for my answers.

MY REFLECTION:

DAY 77
BEING THANKFUL

PHILIPPIANS 4:6

"Be careful for nothing; but in every thing by prayer and supplication with thanksgiving let your requests be made known unto God."

"Be anxious, careful, or take thought of not even one man, woman, or thing; but in all, every and whatsoever thing by earnest prayer and worship, petition or request, with gratitude and thankfulness to God, let the thing you are asking and petitioning for be made known and declared to the supreme Divinity, God." (NWI)

This passage is clear in its directions to us—as well as to the Philippians, to whom Paul was writing this letter. Paul tells the Philippians to not be anxious, or "careful," about anything or anyone. He never said they wouldn't have problems now that they were Christians.

Many times, people are falsely led to believe that once you get saved, you won't ever have another problem. Not only is this not true, it is also completely contrary to what God's Word tells us. I have personally found that the opposite is true. Before we were saved, the devil didn't have to work too hard—we were already on his side. Once we asked Jesus into our hearts, we became the devil's enemy, and the attacks began! The main reason we don't have to be in fear or anxious, though, is because we are not alone in the battle. We now have Jesus to intercede on our behalf when we seek Him.

Paul instructed the Philippians to take their concerns, anxieties and requests and give them all to God, the One who can do what is needed to help, fix, or change things. Being filled with care about someone or something does nothing to change the circumstances except make us basket cases. Paul tells the Philippians to go before God with thankfulness and gratitude for who He is and what He's already done, worshipping Him. Then, we can pray and make our petitions known to Him.

First, we should be thankful, then pray and make our petitions. It sounds simple, and it actually is. The problem arises when we allow the enemy to bring fear and worry into our minds, and we pay attention to those stresses rather than turning them over to the Lord.

Remember, when you find yourself in a difficult place—a loved one is dealing with health issues, you are having marital problems, you have an addictive behavior, or whatever the circumstance might be that's troubling you—stop looking at the problem, get your eyes on Jesus, thank Him for what He has already done for you in other areas of your life, praise Him for who He is, and then seek Him and pray for your needs.

Father, I thank You that You have been faithful to me throughout my life. Thank You for Your love, salvation, peace, hope, and grace. Thank You for all of the times You have been there for me and my family. I come to You for the circumstance that has me troubled and burdened right now. I give it all to You and thank You for answering my prayers, in Jesus' name.

MY REFLECTION:

DAY 78
HOLY IS THE LORD

PSALM 99:3

"Let them praise thy great and terrible name; for it is holy."

*"Let them revere and worship with extended hands and
give thanks to your exceedingly great and reverenced name
of honor and authority; for it is sacred." (NWI)*

Because God is holy, sacred, reverenced, and exceedingly great, we should worship and revere Him. I know the analogy I am about to share has been heard a million times, but it is still very true. If most of us were at a concert watching our favorite singer or band, or if we were at a ballgame featuring our favorite team, or if we saw our favorite famous person, we would be awestruck and our hearts would be racing with excitement. If we were at a concert or game, we would be cheering, screaming, clapping, jumping up and down, and showing our admiration.

That should be our response to the Lord. He created everything we can see or hear, and even things we can't sense because they are so small. God loves us so much that He allowed His Son to come to earth, teach us about the Father's love, grace, mercy and truths, and then die on the cross in a most painful death. Jesus then rose from the grave victoriously in order to save us from eternal separation from God. I don't know of anyone, ever, who even came close to doing all of the above. Surely, God deserves every ounce of praise, gratitude, love and appreciation we have, and we need to express it to Him.

Let me give you another analogy that illustrates this point. What if a friend purchased and gave you a brand new house? You would be so appreciative and thankful to not live in your old, broken-down home that needed a lot of repairs. I imagine you would be thanking, hugging, crying, and laughing with your friend to show your appreciation. Our old "house," that needs lots of repairs because of damage, age, weathering, and usage, was replaced by a brand new house purchased on the cross by Jesus and given to us. It's called salvation, whereby we are "born again" and our "old man" is exchanged for our "new man in Christ." What a glorious gift it is, and God is worthy of all of our praise and worship!

Lord, I pray that I would always recognize Your holiness, Your greatness, and Your authority. I pray that I would come to an understanding of who You are and what You have done for me. When I do, Lord, I will honor, praise, and worship YOU, for You are worthy to receive all glory, honor, and praise.

MY REFLECTION:

DAY 79
BLESSING LEADERS

DEUTERONOMY 1:38

"But Joshua the son of Nun, which stands before thee, he shall go
in thither: encourage him: for he shall cause Israel to inherit it."

Moses led the Israelites out of Egypt according to the intent of the Lord that they would go to the Promised Land. But because of their rebellion, murmuring, and doubt, they didn't get to go in to see God's fullness of blessings for them. So the Lord was going to use Joshua to lead the children of those who came out of Egypt. Moses wasn't even allowed to go because all of their rebellion moved Moses to act out of his flesh rather than trusting the Lord. Since Moses understood the importance of encouragement, which he rarely received from the Israelites, he told the children of Israel to follow Joshua and encourage him.

This is such an important lesson for all of us to learn and remember. Those in leadership desperately need our encouragement. They have a lot of responsibility on their shoulders. They need us to help them, encourage them, support them, pray for them, and bless them. They need those gifts just as much, if not more, than the rest of us, to help them to see the fullness of what God has for them—to help them not quit or be less than they can be.

Whenever you have the opportunity to speak encouragement, bless financially, thank, or help your pastor and his family, please do so. In order for them to lead to their best ability, they need to be lifted up. Show them your support in any way you can. It will enable them to be at their best so that they can bring God's Word faithfully and give love, support, and encouragement to their flock—which, in return, helps us all grow spiritually.

Father, show me ways to help to encourage, strengthen, and lift up those in leadership—especially my pastor. Help me to know specific things to do or say to let them know they are appreciated, loved, and supported.

MY REFLECTION:

DAY 80
BURNING FURNACE

DANIEL 3:25

"He answered and said, Lo, I see four men loose, walking in the midst of the fire, and they have no hurt; and the form of the fourth is like the Son of God."

This passage is referring to 3 young Hebrew men known as Shadrach, Meshach, and Abednego. King Nebuchadnezzar was angry with them because they didn't regard him or his gods and didn't worship the golden image that had been set up. In his fury, he decided if they didn't worship the image, he would have them put in a burning fiery furnace. They told him they trusted God and weren't going to worship the golden image. This made the king even more mad and wanted the furnace to be heated up seven times hotter than it was supposed to be. The furnace was so hot that the men who threw them in were killed. Shadrach, Meshach, and Abednego were tied up, thrown in the furnace, and fell down in the middle of the furnace. All of a sudden, the king looks in and sees four men in there instead of the three. In verse 27 we find out that "the princes, governors, and captains, and the king's counsellors, being gathered together, saw these men, upon whose bodies the fire had no power, nor was an hair of their head singed, neither were their coats changed, nor the smell of fire had passed on them."

Can you imagine the thoughts that must have tormented Shadrach, Meshach, and Abednego upon seeing the very men tossing them into a furnace being burned before they even got in it? It is apparent that their eyes were on the Lord, and not the circumstance that they were facing. Not only did they not get affected by the fire, other than the rope that had them bound was burned off of them, but there was no indication they had even been near a fire.

This is a reminder that if our eyes are fixed on the Lord, He will get us through. The devil can throw all kinds of problems our way, and it may feel like we are going through fire ourselves, but if we keep our eyes on Jesus, He will bring us through just like he did for those three young Hebrew men.

Just like these three could have focused their eyes on the men that were burned in front of them, we can also keep our eyes on the realities of life. If we go through something tragic or difficult, it's sometimes what we think will happen again. Those three chose to trust the Lord and believe for

His protection, but even if they died in the furnace, they still were going to worship the Lord. We need to get our eyes off of former things that have happened and look to God for our hope to do the impossible.

Father, I look to You for my help.

MY REFLECTION:

_____

_____

_____

_____

_____

_____

_____

_____

_____

_____

_____

_____

_____

_____

_____

_____

_____

_____

_____

_____

_____

_____

DAY 81
SHARING OUR TESTIMONY

ACTS 12:17

"But he, beckoning unto them with the hand to hold their peace, declared unto them how the Lord had brought him out of the prison. And he said, Go shew these things unto James and to the brethren. And he departed, and went into another place."

Let's review the account in Acts 12:1-17: Herod had been persecuting, imprisoning, and murdering Christians. He had killed James, the brother of John, and because Herod saw that the Jews were pleased at this, he also put Peter into prison with four quaternions of soldiers guarding him.

Verse 5 says, "Peter therefore was kept in prison: but prayer was made without ceasing of the church unto God for him." Herod had decided to "vex certain of the church."(Acts 12:1) After Easter, Herod planned to bring Peter before the people—similar to what had been done to Jesus. But the entire church prayed without ceasing for Peter (unlike the disciples, who fell asleep while praying for Jesus). The night before Peter was to be brought forth, an angel appeared to him. Peter was soundly sleeping, bound by two chains. Two guards (soldiers) were on either side of him, and there were men who kept the door. This was a seemingly impossible situation! Then, "the angel of the Lord came upon him" (verse 7). When the angel came, "a light shined in the prison," the angel poked Peter in the ribs to wake him up and said, "Arise up quickly."

When Peter rose, his chains fell off his hands. Then, the angel told him to put on clothes and shoes and follow him. Peter followed, but still didn't realize it was an angel. He thought he was having a vision. Peter and the angel passed the first and second ward and came to the iron gate which led to the city. It's important to understand that the iron gate was identified as such because it represents the last difficult thing that seemed impossible to overcome. Iron is extremely heavy—this gate probably would have been too heavy to be opened by Peter alone. But the gate opened by itself!

Neither the angel nor Peter did it. Then, both Peter and the angel went out and passed one street before the angel left (once Peter was safe). Finally, Peter realized what had happened, how God had set him free and delivered him out of the hand of Herod and from all the people of the Jews.

When Peter thought about it, he went to Mary's—John Mark's mother's—house because that was where everyone was gathered in prayer. When Peter first knocked, a girl named Rhoda came to the door and recognized his voice. Instead of opening the door, she ran to tell everyone. The disciples thought she was crazy, but she kept insisting it was Peter. Peter kept knocking. Eventually, they opened the door and were so excited to see him. Peter held up his hand to quiet them and explained how God had delivered him out of prison. Peter told James and his brethren, as well everyone else, to share what had happened.

Let's take a look at some things that are noteworthy about this story:

1) Peter was imprisoned and it seemed like an impossible situation.
2) The church was in constant prayer for him.
3) At the last moment, God intervened.
4) Peter was sleeping, resting, and not worrying.
5) The angel came into the room and brought light. Up until that moment, Peter had been in the dark and couldn't even "see" the impossibility of it all.
6) When Peter obeyed the angel's directions by getting up quickly, his chains fell off his hands.
7) Because the angel knew Peter would be getting out of the prison, he instructed Peter to put on some shoes and clothes—meaning he didn't already have them on.
8) The angel took him past the first and second ward until they came to an iron gate. Sometimes, we are partially freed, but then a seemingly-impossible obstacle appears in front of us to prevent us from being totally delivered. The iron gate would have been too difficult for a weakened man to open by himself, so God supernaturally opened it. God has power over inanimate objects.
9) The angel didn't leave Peter until they were one street past the iron gate, when he was safely freed.
10) When Peter finally realized all the Lord had done to bring him safely out of prison, he immediately went to tell all his friends and fellow believers, who had been praying for him.
11) The young girl that answered Peter's knocking immediately believed it was him, but nobody believed her and thought she was crazy. Her childlike faith enabled her to believe when the others didn't, even though they had been fervently praying for him.
12) It's important to relay our deliverance, and God's supernatural moving in our lives, to other Christians in order to build their faith. Peter told the others to share what had happened. It continued to build their faith to believe the impossible.
13) God made a way where there didn't seem to be any possible way for Peter, and He can do the same for us.
14) Sometimes, we don't realize or recognize what God is doing in our lives until we are set free.

15) Peter went to tell Mary—John Mark's mother—what God had done for him. Usually, there is someone in our lives with whom we want to share the things God has shown us or done for us.

Lord, I pray that I would be bold to share with others what you have done for me, so that their faith can be built to believe You for their impossibilities.

MY REFLECTION:

_____

_____

_____

_____

_____

_____

_____

_____

_____

_____

_____

_____

_____

_____

_____

_____

_____

_____

_____

_____

_____

_____

_____

DAY 82
WHAT WE SPEAK

PSALM 129:8b, c

"The blessing of the Lord be upon you: we bless you in the name of the Lord."

*"The liberal blessing and prosperity of the Eternal Lord be upon you:
we abundantly bless you as a benefit and salute you in the authority,
character and name of the Self-Existent, Eternal, Lord." (NWI)*

It was common in Old Testament times to speak blessings over people—especially over their children. Somewhere in the years since, and especially in modern times, it seems we have gotten away from that practice.

In fact, our mouths actually tend to speak negativity, at times even cursing our situations, ourselves, and our children. I'm not referring to saying curse words; instead, I'm describing the ways we declare things that are bringing about things we really don't want to occur. James 3:10 says, "Out of the same mouth proceedeth blessing and cursing. My brethren, these things ought not so to be." We are speaking things over ourselves, our loved ones, and our situations that are tearing down, bringing hopelessness, causing sickness, and making things less than God intended for them to be.

Repeatedly throughout scripture, we read of the blessings of the Lord for us. There are way too many to name them all here, but to name a few:
- "the blessing of the Lord makes one rich" (Proverbs 10:22, NKJV)
- "blessings are upon the head of the just" (Proverbs 10:6)
- "blessed us with all spiritual blessings" (Ephesians 1:3)
- "[The Lord] will bless us" (Psalm 115:12)
- "blessed shalt thou be in the city, and blessed shalt thou be in the field" (Deuteronomy 28:3)
- "pour you out a blessing" (Malachi 3:10)

Let's begin speaking blessings over people and situations rather than speaking curses over them. Let's speak God's Word over our children and our situations—scriptures that declare God's love, provision, guidance, wisdom, help, direction, deliverance, peace, and salvation. Instead of declaring what we see, what we don't want, or what we are afraid of, let's start declaring what God wants and start blessing ourselves and others in order to see God's blessing be poured out.

Father, help me watch my words so that they will line up with Your Words. Help me declare Your promises rather than what I am afraid will happen. Help me believe what You say instead of what I might see or hear. Let my words bring life, hope, peace, joy, encouragement, wisdom, and all that You have for us, in Jesus' name.

MY REFLECTION:

DAY 83
GOD SURPRISES

PSALM 90:17

"And the beauty of the Lord our God be upon us: and establish thou the work of our hands upon us; yea, the work of our hands establish thou it."

As I was looking at a ring I usually wear on my right ring finger, I remembered when I'd bought it. It was a situation that turned out to be totally unexpected.

Typically, I wear a ring that is durable, that I can leave on my finger without worrying about damaging it. I have a number of rings I wear to match an outfit if I'm doing something special; but for day-to-day use, I keep a ring on my right ring finger that I don't have to take off every time I'm working, digging, or cleaning. The ring I used to wear was sterling silver with a black onyx stone. I wear a good amount of black clothing, so it was practical. I wore this ring for 15 years or more until, one day, I noticed the stone was missing. I had no idea when it had happened, let alone where it was. It wasn't an expensive ring, but I really liked it, so I was quite disappointed.

I had no idea how difficult it was to find another simple ring—not too big or too small, inexpensive, sterling silver with a black onyx. I searched for a couple of years until, one day, my husband and I were on vacation in Maine. We went into a small antique shop. I asked the lady if she had any black onyx rings. We actually found one that fit, was my style and size, and that I liked. I was thrilled to find that it was also in my price range (did I mention that I'm cheap when it comes to buying things for myself?).

So I bought it. When we returned to the car, I noticed it looked different in the sunlight compared to the dark, low-lit store. Being on vacation, I hadn't brought anything to clean jewelry with, so I improvised with a cotton swab and toothpaste. It didn't get all the dirt and grime off, but it did get the ring clean enough for me to see that this was more than I thought. When we arrived home, I was so excited to use my jewelry cleaner. I discovered that my $30 sterling silver black onyx ring was in actuality an emerald sitting on filigreed gold and silver with very small diamonds on each side.

What?

Why the antique shop had never tried to clean it was a mystery to me; but it turned out to be a huge blessing. I've never had it appraised, except for a jeweler confirming that it was a real emerald—not man-made.

As I looked at this ring, I marveled at the fact that, when I purchased it, everyone—the shop-keeper, my husband and myself—thought it was black onyx. It was so dirty you couldn't see the emerald, the gold or the small diamonds. Only with some "elbow grease" was the true gem discovered. This caused me to wonder what other gems are discarded because they are "dirty."

God has created us just like that emerald: to glisten and display our beauty; but if we are covered in the dirt and grime of everyday life, no one will see how beautiful we truly are. People may even assume we're not who we really are! Are we so disguised and damaged because of our surroundings or sins that we are unrecognizable as Christians? Just like I cleaned this ring only to discover the real gem and value, God wants to clean us up, too. He wants to get rid of the dirt and grime—to expose who we really are so that we can be appreciated for who we really are.

Ezekiel 28:13 says that emeralds were one of the precious stones "in Eden the garden of God." Revelation 4:3 says that God's glory is "like a jasper and a sardine stone: and there was a rainbow round about the throne, in sight like unto an emerald." In Revelation 21, John "saw a new heaven and a new earth," "the holy city, new Jerusalem, coming down from God out of heaven, prepared as a bride adorned for her husband," "and the foundations of the wall of the city were garnished with all manner of precious stones," "the fourth, an emerald."

It seems to me that God blessed me that day: not only did I receive an emerald ring, but it is a stone named in the Bible from Eden to New Jerusalem. What special blessing does God have for you? What "surprise" is hidden until you take the time to discover it? God wants to bless us. He wants to expose "beauty from ashes." He wants to take what has been inside you all along and clean it up to reveal the beautiful gem that you are.

Father, help me to become the gem You created me to be. Help me to allow You to "clean me up" so that I might glisten for You.

MY REFLECTION:

DAY 84

ACCEPTING GOD'S MERCY

JONAH 2:8

"They that observe lying vanities forsake their own mercy."

"They that observe, regard, take heed or keep guile, idolatry, is false, lying and vain in their actions, words or deeds, forsake and relinquish their own favor, mercy, kindness, and pity." (NWI)

First of all, what is mercy?

According to the Hebrew in this verse, *mercy* means, "kindness, favor, good deed, loving kindness, kindness, pity and reproach." I don't know about you, but I need all of God's mercy. I need God to be kind and show me favor. I need Him to give me pity when I'm going through a tough time. Of course, no one ever wants to be reproached, but it's nice to know that, if I've gotten off course, my heavenly Father loves me enough to correct me so that I can get back to where I need to be.

But according to this verse, it's quite clear that we can actually relinquish our mercy by being false, vain, idolatrous, or liars. If that doesn't convince me to be the opposite of those traits, I don't know what will. It seems in today's world that people not only exhibit these traits—they are comfortable doing them. It makes me ponder how many of God's blessings we aren't able to have because we decide to lie, have false gods, are deceiving, and are vain.

Notice that I said "decided." Once again, we can choose to tell lies, be vain, have other gods in our lives, and be deceitful—or choose *not* to do those things. Not only do we make these decisions, but it also appears that we choose to "keep" them in our lives (meaning we can choose to stop doing them and return to the Lord).

Our loving Heavenly Father desires to bless us and give us mercy, but we may not be able to receive all He wants to extend to us because of our own choices. It reminds me of a parent/child relationship. As a parent, I may want to bless my son or daughter with a car when they turn 16 or give my younger child a toy he or she has been deeply longing to have; but if I continuously see my child acting in a way that shows they can't be trusted to use the object properly, I probably won't give them their desired gift until they change their ways. We need to see that they have integrity when we aren't with them as well as when we are right beside them. Can we trust them to be honest? Can we trust them not to try to wiggle out of trouble by being deceitful ? If the toy was broken or the car was in an accident, would they be up-front and honest about what happened so that we can show them pity? If this is so, our hearts are open to pour out favor, mercy, kindness, and pity.

God's desire is to "be there for us," whether to show us His love and kindness, to help us in difficult situations or to comfort us through trials. Let's choose to walk in integrity and trustworthiness, honestly serving the Lord. If we do, we will be open to receive God's mercy. Sure, He may need to reproach us from time to time, like the father does his son if he causes an accident in his new car; but reproach comes out of God's lovingkindness. He has our best interests at heart.

Thank You, Lord, for Your mercy that You give when I need Your comfort, kindness, favor and even reproach. Thank You, Father, that Your heart is to show me Your mercy. Forgive me when I have relinquished all You wanted to do for me because I kept guile, idolatry, lying, and vanity in my life. Show me, Lord, how to turn those traits over to You and decide to not behave in those ways anymore, that I might receive Your favor.

MY REFLECTION:

_____

_____

_____

_____

_____

_____

_____

_____

_____

_____

_____

DAY 85
PAY ATTENTION

COLOSSIANS 4:17

"And say to Archippus, Take heed in the ministry which
thou hast received in the Lord, that thou fulfil it."

*"And to Archippus, tell by word or writing, to take heed, beware,
and perceive in regard to the office, service, and ministry which
you have received in the Lord, that you execute the office,
finish the task, fully preach, and accomplish it." (NWI)*

Even though this passage is directed to Archippus, I believe Paul would tell us all the same thing. We should pay attention and regard what God has put in our lives as ministry, to be sure to do all He wants us to do and not quit before He says to quit. Until our season of that ministry is over, we should continue doing what God has told us to do, knowing He still has a purpose for our being there.

We may, at times, be tired of what we're doing; things may get difficult; we may be frustrated; we may see other ministries as more interesting. But no matter how tempted we may be to give up doing what God has told us to do, we should never quit until we hear God's instructions to do something else.

I distinctly remember a job situation I didn't want to stay in, but I knew without a shadow of a doubt that God ordered my steps there. He'd proven it several times over. Because of many problems associated with that position—struggles that came from my boss, coworkers, and others—I wanted desperately to quit. But as badly as I wanted to be out of there, I knew God hadn't released me yet. I honestly can't tell you that I was always a happy camper about it. God knew the reason I was there, even if I didn't. During my last week at that job, I was able to lead someone to the Lord. If for no other reason, I was to stay for that one person to be saved.

I know the Lord used me for other reasons, as well, and used others as lifelong friends and sisters in Christ for me. I will never forget the importance of staying until God says "go." We don't always understand why God has us somewhere. It doesn't always make sense to our natural minds. But we need to remember that God's ways aren't our ways, and He has us where we are for a reason bigger than we can possibly imagine.

As difficult as it may be sometimes, it's important to continue doing the last thing we know God told us to do until He releases us from it. We have no idea how He may want to use us for His kingdom.

Father, forgive me for the times I've quit doing something You weren't ready for me to leave. Help me understand the principle of staying until I hear otherwise from You. Help me, Lord, to be patient—to listen to Your voice and Your timing. Lead me, speak to me and assure me, that I might know Your will.

MY REFLECTION:

DAY 86
PRAISE

PSALM 145:4

"One generation shall praise thy works to another,
and shall declare thy mighty acts."

PSALM 78:4, 6

"We will not hide them from their children, shewing to the generation to come
the praises of the Lord, and his strength, and his wonderful works that he hath
done. . . . That the generation to come might know them, even the children
which should be born; who should arise and declare them to their children."

I pray you are as challenged by these verses as I am today. What are we telling our children—and any children we are privileged to be in contact with—about God? Are we sharing with them about His goodness to us, His love for us, His promises over us, His salvation? Are we sharing with them that He is a jealous God that desires our worship and praise? Do we share with them His exploits? How will the next generation—and those after—know about God unless we tell them?

Has God comforted you, healed you, protected you, saved you, delivered you, or provided for you? Then you should tell your children, grandchildren, your neighbor's children, nieces, nephews, and any other children in your life, so they can understand and also share the goodness of God. I can without a doubt testify to so many blessings God has given me. I'm sure we all can. But we need to share these with the next generations so they can experience His strength, love, hope, joy, peace, and all of His mighty acts. Then, they can do likewise and share what God has done for them, reaching the generations in the future that we can't personally reach.

Lord, thank You for all You have done for me, from providing beautiful
sunrises and sunsets to providing for my needs—and all Your
other many blessings. Remind me, please, to share Your abundant

goodness with others, but especially with the younger generation, that they might also see and understand Your goodness.

MY REFLECTION:

_____

_____

_____

_____

_____

_____

_____

_____

_____

_____

_____

_____

_____

_____

_____

_____

_____

_____

_____

_____

_____

_____

_____

_____

DAY 87

RUNNING THE RACE

HEBREWS 12:1

"... let us lay aside every weight, and the sin which doth so easily beset us, and let us run with patience the race that is set before us."

We are all in races. Just as Track and Field races are of various lengths, so are our spiritual races. For us to effectively run the races of our life and to be the most refreshed to do them, we must center our lives around Jesus. True refreshment that will keep us going, keep us healthy and strong, and keep us focused, must come from time spent with the Lord.

There are many ways to get refreshed. You might go on a vacation, get away for the day, talk to a friend, take a nap, go to church, read a good book, listen to music, take a walk, work out at the gym, or get some ice cream. They are only temporary fixes and as helpful as they may be at the moment, none of those will give you the refreshing that is needed to "keep going" when life's struggles are heavier than you can carry.

The only enduring refreshment and ability to stay through life's day-to-day grind as well difficulties, is to spend time with the Lord in prayer and worship and lean on Jesus when things get tough. Our own capabilities and our confidence in them produce even more stress in our lives because we don't have what it takes to successfully finish the races set before us.

The races we face will be different, depending on the season we are in, but will look something like these:

Short sprints or dashes: taking food to someone sick, taking the kids to an amusement park, doing errands, a cold, keeping the nursery at church quarterly.

Relay races: Teaching Sunday school or Bible Study, working at a job, moving to a new city or home/apartment before you settle in one place, learning how to get along with co-workers, neighbors, students, spouses, children, family, or friends.

Hurdles: bad health diagnosis, losing a job, spouse leaves you, death of a loved one.

Mile: commitments that are on-going, being room parent, visiting a nursing home weekly, cutting a neighbor's yard every week, taking someone to church that couldn't go otherwise, .

Marathon: marriages, ministries, children, jobs, taking care of family members, promises that God spoke to you but haven't yet come to fruition.

Triathlon: multi-tasking, being called on to fulfill many things at once (parent, spouse, having a job, caregiver, coaching, playing sports, student)

Hebrews 12:2 indicates that the way to deal with all that we must go through is by "Looking unto Jesus, the author and finisher of our faith". In and of ourselves we aren't able to endure everything that comes our way with peace, but Philippians 4:13 declares, "I can do all things through Christ which strengtheneth me." Notice, Christ is the One giving me the strength to do all things. Now that is a source of refreshment!

Lord, help me to lean on You when I am weak and not feel
like I can finish the race that's before me on my own.

MY REFLECTION:

DAY 88
CHOICES

PSALM 37:39

"But the salvation of the righteous is of the Lord:
he is their strength in the time of need."

In Psalm 37, we see many things in life that we have a choice to do or not do. Let's take a look at them:

1) "Fret not thyself because of evildoers . . . "
2) "Neither be thou envious . . . "
3) "Trust in the Lord . . . "
4) "Do good . . . "
5) "Delight thyself also in the Lord . . . "
6) "Commit thy way unto the Lord . . . "
7) "Trust also in him . . . "
8) "Rest in the Lord, and wait patiently for him . . . "
9) "Fret not thyself because of him who prospereth in his way . . . "
10) "Cease from anger . . . "
11) "Forsake wrath . . . "
12) "Fret not thyself in any wise to do evil . . . "
13) "The meek . . . shall delight themselves in the abundance of peace . . . "
14) "Depart from evil . . . "
15) "Do good . . . "
16) "Dwell for evermore . . . "
17) "Wait on the Lord . . . "
18) "Keep his way . . . "

There are 18 things listed that we need to decide to do. Notice that several are repeated. Anytime God repeats something, it means we need to pay extra attention to it. God told us twice "to do good" and to "trust the Lord." He reminded us three times to "fret not thyself." All three of these are good reminders. Fretting certainly doesn't help us at all, and in fact only makes us full of anxiety, worry and fear. On the contrary, when we trust the Lord and do good, we are building our strength, encouragement, hope and faith. If we choose to do these things, we will be free and live abundant lives. If we choose to not do them, it will keep us in bondage.

Now, let's look at some specific benefits to deciding to follow God's ways that are named in this psalm:

- We don't need to worry or be envious of evildoers because they will be "cut down like the grass, and wither."
- If we will trust in the Lord and do good, we will "dwell in the land" and "be fed."
- If we'll delight ourselves in the Lord, He'll "give thee the desires of thine heart."
- When we commit our way to the Lord and trust Him, "he shall bring it to pass."
- "Those that wait upon the Lord, they shall inherit the earth."
- When we depart from evil, the Lord "forsaketh not his saints."
- "The righteous will inherit the land, and dwell therein forever." When we wait on the Lord and keep His way . . . "He will exalt thee to inherit the land," and we'll see the wicked cut off.

As I stated earlier, these are moment-by-moment decisions we must make. If we choose to follow God's advice in this psalm, we will live abundant lives, have the fruit of the Spirit, and walk in His strength and ability and not our own.

Thank You, Lord, for showing me the benefits of decisions made to trust you, rest in You, wait on You, dwell with You, delight in You and do good. You are faithful, Lord! Help me choose daily to follow You and Your Word, that I may live a life full of all that You have for me.

MY REFLECTION:

DAY 89
CO-HEIRS

I PETER 2:9

"But ye are a chosen generation, a royal priesthood, an holy nation,
a peculiar people: that ye should shew forth the praises of him
who hath called you out of darkness into his marvellous light."

*"But you have been exceedingly, abundantly chosen from where you were in
your diversity and kindred, a kingly, powerful, priest, an holy, pure, blameless
and consecrated race, even though you aren't Jewish, an abundant people
for a purpose and intent, that you should celebrate the praises and excellence
of Jesus who has called you by your name out of obscurity and darkness
into His wonderful, marvelous light that shines like manifesting rays." (NWI)*

I don't think we fully comprehend what Jesus has done for those of us who were not born Jewish. By His death and resurrection, He paid the way for those who were not born Jewish to become family—and even more than that, to become chosen, pure, and blameless.

He enabled us to become co-heirs with Himself as a royal priest by personally calling us by name. Yes, He knows our name! When we accept Jesus as our Lord and Savior, it is more than just getting our "ticket" to heaven. It also includes all the rights and privileges of being a son or daughter of the Most High God. No matter what we did previously, He forgave us and made us holy, pure and blameless. As royal priests, we now have the power and authority of the King of kings. No matter who or where we came from, we have now become righteous. We used to be foreigners, but now we are sons and daughters with a purpose.

Because of what He has done for us, we should celebrate and praise Him for bringing us out of the obscure darkness we used to be in and into His marvelous, beautiful light.

Lord, thank You so much for all You have done for me. Thank You
for transforming and changing me from darkness to Your light.

MY REFLECTION:

DAY 90
THE THIEF

JOHN 10:10

"The thief cometh not, but for to steal, and to kill, and to destroy: I am come that they might have life, and that they might have it more abundantly."

Early one morning, I went to the beach. For about 20 minutes, I was all by myself, and the Lord showed me something I believe has a spiritual connection and understanding to it.

At first, I was solely concentrating on the numerous turtle nests down the beach from us, trying to figure out the codes on the marker sticks and see the nest where, a few nights prior, we'd watched a sea turtle laying her eggs. Because my focus was zeroed in, I completely missed everything going on around me. I walked back to our resort and decided to stand there, looking out at the Gulf. I was so excited and blessed by what I saw.

Initially, I had a sweet time with the Lord—I was just singing and praising God. At some point, I began praying in the Spirit and crying before the Lord, pouring out my heart and giving Him my concerns and prayers. As I stood there, a young man, probably in his 30s, went down to the water's edge to fish. I continued singing, praying, and observing. When I looked out at the expanse of the Gulf, I could see a dolphin swimming. Shortly afterwards, I saw several dolphins swimming—three pods of them. Occasionally, I would see something feeding out in the deeper waters.

As serene, peaceful, and beautiful as it all was, something occurred that brought my spiritual antennas up. The fisherman was standing shin-deep in the water, but his gear was behind him, about 30 feet away from the incoming tide. It appeared safe, but in actuality, it wasn't. The eye-opening experience was very simple. I observed the man attentively fishing, but paying no mind or thought to anything but what was right in front of him. A crow flew down, grabbed one of his bags and flew off with it. It was a bright yellow bag—from where I was standing at the top of the beach, I could tell there was something inside. I didn't know what. I went down to tell the man, but he just said, "That's okay," and turned around to continue fishing.

I went back to the top of the beach, pondering what had occurred. The crow came back and picked up another bag, but maybe it was too heavy, because this time, he didn't carry it away. As I reflected on all of this, it reminded me of how we can be like that fisherman. We may be so focused on doing a specific task that we miss seeing God's beauty, His blessings, and the thieves that take away our possessions when we're not looking. What the crow "stole" may not have been valuable in the fisherman's opinion, but there was no way of knowing when he would need it again. Perhaps he had extra hooks in the bag, or weights. He may have had a harder time fishing on his next trip because of the lack of that bag.

I wonder how many times this has happened in my own life. Have I been so focused on doing something—even the Lord's work—that I have been oblivious to "the thief" stealing from me? At the time, someone may have had to tell me what happened for me to even realize it. Maybe I dismissed it as not being important enough to worry about, when in actuality, what I allowed to be taken from me was preventing me from doing all God had for me. Who knows what "big one" got away because I was now missing the equipment needed for the job?

Lord, help me to be present with You, and to share Your spiritual vision. Help me to see Your beauty, as well to be observant of what is trying to be taken from me. Help me to take it seriously and not shrug it off, so that I can chase it away in the name of Jesus. Let me see with Your eyes, Lord.

MY REFLECTION:

_____

_____

_____

_____

_____

_____

_____

_____

_____

_____

_____

_____

_____

DAY 91
GLORY

PSALM 96:8a

"Give unto the LORD the glory due unto his name. . . ."

I'm sure I'm not alone in saying that I'm much more apt to give God my prayer requests, hurts and wants than I am "the glory due His name." This realization truly made me stop, rest in Him, take a deep breath and glorify Him.

He has been so amazing and faithful in my life. Glorifying Him should be my first response; but sadly, that isn't always the case. Has my life been a bed of roses? Definitely not! But has God shown Himself to be bigger than any problems I have faced? Most definitely! He has been my Healer, Deliverer, Friend, Comforter, Savior, Peace that passes understanding, Provider, Hope, Joy, Strength, Husband, Father, Love, and anything and everything I have ever needed.

Through everything that has taken me back a few steps, everything that has blessed me, everything that has hurt me, everything that has brought sadness, doubt, fear, anger, pain, discouragement, grief, sickness and disease, failure, broken promises, guilt, and so much more, He has never left me nor forsaken me. He may not have answered right away, or how I would have liked, but His answers were always for my good, filled with grace and mercy, and always came just when I needed them.

But even more than all He has done for me personally, I am grateful and I honor Him for all He has done to make our world so beautiful. He gives us the sun to provide warmth and light, clouds to keep us from burning up, a moon and stars to light up our night sky, water to quench our thirst, delicious and varied food, rainbows to remind of us His promise to us, aromatic flowers and plants that are intricately designed and fashioned, animals that are distinct, beautiful and purposeful, friends and family, and so much more. He has given us a mind to create and think, senses to enjoy His creation, emotions to express our feelings, and a beautiful place to live.

The earth is so diverse—every type of biome from rivers, streams, ponds, lakes, oceans, seas, and waterfalls to deserts, mountains, canyons, mesas, rain forests, plateaus, swamps, valleys, and forests. There are not enough words to express my gratitude for all He has given to me to enjoy. I have the ability to feel His presence, and He has made known to me His blessings. I just want to praise Him, thank Him and give Him the glory and honor due His name, because He is truly *worthy of all praise*!

Thank You, Lord, for Your goodness, grace and mercy. I honor You today, and I give You the glory that is truly due Your name. You are worthy, Lord, of all glory, honor, and praise. Help me to always remember Your goodness to me rather than keeping my eyes only on my problems. I love You, Lord.

MY REFLECTION:

DAY 92
THANKFUL

I THESSALONIANS 5:18

"In everything give thanks: for this is the will of
God in Christ Jesus concerning you."

Paul didn't say we should just be thankful in the good times, when we are healthy, when our finances are good, when our marriage is wonderful, or when our children do well—although we should of course be thankful for all of those things and so much more. But Paul says, "In everything"!

What does that mean exactly? It means we should be thankful for everything—the blessings and even the negative things. Why? Why would Paul tell us to be thankful for bad news, unruly kids, death, an unfaithful spouse, health issues, a lost job, or unfulfilled dreams? Is he saying we should thank God for cancer, going bankrupt, being sexually or physically abused, a robbery, loss of a loved one, or ruined family lives because of addictions? I think Paul was trying to tell us that we should thank God because we can trust Him to bring us through our difficulties. We're not thanking Him *for* the problems, but we're thanking Him that He has a bigger plan than we can understand at that moment. God can see the ultimate purpose and plan that we can't see yet.

A perfect example from God's Word is the story of Joseph from Genesis 37-50. He was one of Jacob's 12 sons and was his Father's favorite. Joseph had dreams that made his brothers mad, so they decided they would make it seem he had been attacked and eaten by animals, but they actually sold him into slavery. Many things happened to him during his time of slavery, including being imprisoned, but God's favor was with him and he ultimately became second in command under Pharaoh. God used Joseph to interpret Pharoah's dreams, by which it was revealed there would be 7 years of plenty, followed by 7 years of famine. When things got really bad because of the lack of food, Jacob sent his other sons to Egypt to get food, not knowing they would be dealing with Joseph. At first, Joseph didn't let them know who he was, but finally, after many encounters, the whole family was reunited and provided for throughout the famine. Joseph could not possibly have known or understood when he was sold into slavery, that God would bless him and use him mightily to provide for his family.

When we are thanking Him, we are recognizing that He is going to somehow make the horrible situations in our lives turn out okay—and even more, that He is going to bring good out of it all. We can thank Him for being a loving, faithful, merciful, gracious, compassionate, forgiving, saving Heavenly Father. We can thank Him for being faithful to always bring us through difficulties, past, present, and future. We can thank Him that He is a way-maker. We can thank Him that Isaiah 53:4a says, "Surely he hath born our griefs, and carried our sorrows . . . " and verse 5 says, "But he was wounded for our transgressions, he was bruised for our iniquities: the chastisement of our peace was upon him; and with his stripes we are healed."

Jesus was acquainted with sorrow and grief. He bore everything we would go through when He died on the cross so that He could fully understand our pains and feel our hurts. Since He understands, He is faithful to help us, carry us if needed and bring us through it all.

So yes, we can give thanks to God for everything!

Father, help me to be ever mindful of Your love for me—the truth that You would allow Your only Son Jesus to die for my sins, that I might live eternally with You. Thank You for always being faithful to bring my situations to victory, no matter how difficult the circumstances may be. Thank You for Your love, mercy, and grace. THANK YOU!

MY REFLECTION:

_____

_____

_____

_____

_____

_____

_____

_____

_____

_____

_____

_____

DAY 93
BLESSING

PSALM 55:22

"Cast thy burden upon the Lord, and he shall sustain thee:
he shall never suffer the righteous to be moved."

"Throw away and even hurl what has been given to you by the Eternal Lord, to Him, and He will provide sustenance, be able to guide you, be present and be able to bear you: He will never cause, ordain, or deliver the righteous to waver, be carried out of course, to fall in decay, shaken, or be removed." (NWI)

My previous understanding of this verse was that, if I give God my problems, He'll help me and not let me be moved by them. I'm not saying that's wrong, but as I looked up the words in Hebrew, I discovered a deeper, very exciting meaning.

God blesses us so that we can be a blessing to someone else. So when God blesses us, rather than merely using those blessings for ourselves, we should "give them back" to Him. He is allowing us the privilege of using them, because everything belongs to Him. We need to realize that we are just stewards of what He has given us.

With that in mind, when God blesses us, we should obviously acknowledge His gifts to us, but in addition, we should give them back to Him. As this wording says, we should throw them back to Him. In my mind, I envision it like a batter hitting a baseball to the shortstop—and as soon as he gets it, he throws it immediately, as hard and fast as he can, to the first baseman to get the out. We are to do the same: we give our blessings immediately back to the Lord to see how they can best be used.

The amazing thing is that, if we'll give our blessings and gifts back to God, He will not only use them to help others but also use them to help us. Scripture says He will provide sustenance, He'll guide, He'll be present, and He'll bear us up. In other words, He'll take care of every need we have.

That in and of itself is awesome, but He's not done there. In addition, it says that He will never cause, deliver or ordain anything that would cause us to be shaken, removed, to fall in decay, or to be carried out of course. In other words, He'll keep us on track and make sure we stand against anything that tries to bring us down. Glory to God! One key fact in all of this is that we must be willing to give what He has given to us *back* to Him—our marriage, our children, our job, our finances, our health . . . everything He has given us! If God has blessed you with children, dedicate and give them back to the Giver of Life. If God has given you money, a spouse, a job, health . . . give it all to Him, that He can use these things for His glory. When we do so, He will "supply all your need according to His riches in glory by Christ Jesus" (Philippians 4:19).

Lord, help me give back to You the blessings You have graciously given me, that You can do amazing things through those blessings. Help me to understand that the principle of giving blessings back to You is Your way of providing for and blessing me even further, in Jesus's name.

MY REFLECTION:

DAY 94
ON HOLD

I THESSALONIANS 5:24

"Faithful is he that calleth you, who also will do it."

"Trustworthy, faithful, sure, and true is He that calls you by your name, who also will appoint, bring forth, perform, provide, purpose, and execute it without any delay." (NWI)

Sometimes, it seems that God puts things on hold. I know I've experienced this in my own life on multiple occasions. Things I have asked God for—things I felt the Lord spoke to me, or things I am believing for loved ones—almost appear to fall on deaf ears as I wait, and wait, and then wait some more.

An interesting portion of this verse indicates that God calls us by our names. That is a very personal, intimate relationship. Because of our relation to the Lord, He will bring to pass that which He has called you to do.

One specific prayer I had been praying for and believing God for over 45 years still had not come to pass. On a number of occasions, I thought I had misunderstood what God had told me and would give up, only to feel God "pull me back" to believe for what I so strongly thought He'd spoken to me. Nonetheless, for over 45 years, I was trusting God to do what only He could do. It was definitely much more than I could do in my own strength. Yet it still wasn't God's timing for it to come to pass . . . *until it was*! When we continue to trust our ever-faithful Heavenly Father, He will perform His Word, answer our prayers, make a way where there doesn't seem to be a way, and He will do it without delay.

Decades ago, a friend of mine gave me a scripture on a Christmas present she made. It was a heart-shaped ornament on which she wrote Habakkuk 2:2-3: "And the LORD answered me, and said, Write the vision, and make it plain upon tables, that he may run that readeth it. For the vision is yet for an appointed time, but at the end it shall speak, and not lie: though it tarry, wait for it; because it will surely come, it will not tarry." When she gave it to me, it was special because she lovingly made it for me. It wasn't until years later that I realized that it referred to the specific thing for which I was believing God.

At first glance, the passage almost seems contradictory to itself. But upon further investigation, it all made sense. When we are praying or believing for something, it sometimes seems like forever before we get our answer. And then, *boom*, all of a sudden something happens that lets us know God has been working behind the scenes all along. "Though it tarry, wait for it; because it will surely come, it will not tarry." So we wait for it, and God, in His appointed time, will bring it forth and execute it. Psalm 27:14 says, "Wait on the LORD, be of good courage, and he shall strengthen thine heart: wait, I say, on the LORD."

Father, as I await the ministry or calling You have for me, help me to be patient and not give up before Your appointed timing. Help me, Lord, to recognize Your voice so that I will be obedient to listen to it as You lead and guide me. Thank You, Lord, that I can trust You to bring it to pass.

MY REFLECTION:

DAY 95

CONFIDENCE IN THE LORD

PROVERBS 29:25b

" . . . but whoso putteth his trust in the Lᴏʀᴅ shall be safe."

" . . . but inasmuch as you certainly, rightly, and doubtless put your bold, confident and secure hope and trust in the Lord, you will be safe, strong and inaccessible." (NWI)

G od's Word says we are to "come boldly unto the throne of grace, that we may obtain mercy, and find grace to help in time of need" (Hebrews 4:16).Proverbs 3:26 says, "For the Lᴏʀᴅ shall be thy confidence, and shall keep thy foot from being taken." God's Word is full of His promises that declare He will provide for us if we trust and have faith in Him. He will provide His deliverance, salvation, faith, protection, healing, peace, comfort, joy, provision, and grace.

Based on Proverbs 3:26, even our confidence comes from Him. When we trust Him, believe Him, honor Him, and have faith in who He is, what He has done, what He is doing, and what He will do, God keeps us from going astray or getting out of His will. We may not understand everything that's going on—we may not like what is happening to us or to a loved one—but we can be sure that, if we keep our hope and trust in Him, He will cause us to be safe and be stronger than we imagined we could be. All we need to do is trust Him through our circumstances.

> Father, I know You only want what is best for me and my loved ones. Help me to put my trust and confidence in You and You alone. Help me to not doubt, be afraid, or worry, because if I turn my eyes away from the circumstances and keep them on You, I know You will keep me safe.

MY REFLECTION:

DAY 96
PREPARATION

EPHESIANS 6:10-18

"Finally, my brethren, be strong in the Lord, and in the power of his might. Put on the whole armour of God, that ye may be able to stand against the wiles of the devil. . . . Stand therefore, having your loins girt about with truth, and having on the breastplate of righteousness; And your feet shod with the preparation of the gospel of peace . . . shield of faith . . . helmet of salvation, and the sword of the Spirit . . . praying always . . ."

In God's Word, I have noticed the importance of being prepared. I have heard it said that, by being prepared, we are blessed. Even though it is very true, this might be misunderstood to merely mean that God gives us all kinds of money, possessions, and other desires of our hearts. While God does pour out His blessings on those who seek Him, those blessings might come in different forms than prosperity. For instance, we can be blessed with God's protection, healing, good grades in school, wisdom, His grace and mercy, a good marriage, children and grandchildren that love the Lord, deliverance from addictions, peace, faith, and so on.

Because we have prepared our ways before the Lord, we can relate to 2 Chronicles 27:6 where it says "Jotham [we] became mighty [strengthened, helped, repaired, constant, encouraged, maintained, mighty, prevailing, recovered, withstanding]". In other words, because Jotham prepared his ways, God blessed him.

Then again, if we don't prepare our hearts to seek the Lord, we could become like Rehoboam in 2 Chronicles 12:14, where king Rehoboam did not prepare his ways before the Lord his God and did evil (bad, adversity, affliction, calamity, distress, grief, harm, heavy, mischief, misery, sorrow, trouble, wickedness, wrong). We may think to ourselves that we could never do something like becoming addicted, having an affair, hurting someone, not going to church, becoming prideful, or walking away from the Lord; but if we do not purposefully prepare our hearts to seek God continually, we can easily fall into the devil's traps.

All of this brings me to my final point: what are we doing to be prepared for the coming of the Lord? It is quite obvious that prophecy has been and is being fulfilled daily. Difficult times are predicted in God's Word, and unless we have prepared our hearts to seek God—His wisdom, His guidance, and His face—we will be afraid, anxious, confused, worried, and we won't make wise decisions.

I remember being in school and having fire drills and tornado drills. They were designed to prepare us on the off chance that an emergency occurred. They prepared everyone to know what to do in case something happened—fear would be lessened, purpose would be natural, and everyone would be calm enough to listen to instructions.

How can we be prepared? First and foremost, if you haven't already done so, ask Jesus to be your Lord and Savior, and be prepared to stand up for Him no matter the cost. Then, seek first the kingdom of God, forgive others, stay humble before the Lord, read His Word, pray, listen to His still, small voice, and be ready to help others in need so that you can be led by the Holy Spirit (the Teacher giving us instructions in case of an emergency).

Lord, show me how to be prepared. As I seek first Your kingdom, I lean on You to show me what I need to do. Thank You, Lord, for preparing me.

MY REFLECTION:

_____

_____

_____

_____

_____

_____

_____

_____

_____

_____

_____

_____

_____

_____

DAY 97
TRUST

PSALM 43:5

"Why are you cast down, O my soul? And why art thou disquieted within me? Hope in God: for I shall yet praise him, who is the health of my countenance, and my God."

The psalmist David had his fair share of difficult circumstances—on many occasions, these trials brought him to despair. Yet over and over, David came to the realization that he needed to consciously decide to stop looking at the problems. He was reminded continually that God would be his hope and the health to his countenance.

So many times, we get discouraged, disappointed, frustrated, or depressed because of situations that may not go the way we'd hoped. We may have health, financial, family, business, relationship, or other problems that send us into a tailspin. I realize that some people have chemical imbalances, extenuating circumstances, PTSD, and other conditions that may require medical help; but for the rest of us, it boils down to a choice we must make to trust and put our hope in the Lord rather than fret over our problems. Worry, anxiety, fear, and discouragement do not help us at all—in actuality, they make things worse. However, turning our problem(s) over to the Lord brings hope and encouragement. We must make a conscious decision to hand the problems to the Lord and trust Him.

There have been times I've been so overwhelmed with conditions and situations in my life that I literally would stand with my hand lifted to the Lord, as if I was handing it to Him. It was my way of releasing control of my concerns to the only One who could actually do something to change the circumstances. It was taking my hands off the things that had me fearful, worried, and depressed, and giving those things to the Lord.

We need to remember that He is ever-faithful to fulfill His promises and be a "very present help in trouble. Therefore, will not we fear . . . . The Lord of hosts is with us; the God of Jacob is our refuge" (Psalm 46:1, 2a, 7).

Oh Father, as I surrender my concerns, worries, anxieties, fears, and problems to You, I let go of trying to manipulate, control, and figure out everything. I am asking You to help me trust You, as I know You are much more capable of handling my problem than I am. Thank You, Lord, for how You are going to answer my prayer. Thank You for Your faithfulness. Thank You for Your peace. Thank You for Your hope.

MY REFLECTION:

DAY 98
FAITH

HEBREWS 11:1
"Now faith is the substance of things hoped for,
the evidence of things not seen."

"Moreover, your conviction of the truthfulness of God, and reliance upon Christ for salvation, health and deliverance, and your inward certainty, is the setting to support your assurance and confidence of the matter expected, anticipated and trusted for, the proof, conviction and report (announcement) of matters not perceived or beheld yet, but will be made fertile and bring forth abundantly." (NWI)

When we believe God's Word as truth—when we rely on Christ for our salvation, health, and deliverance, and we are certain about these things—that is the basis (support) for our assurance and confidence. That's what allows us to believe that what we're expecting from God will happen in abundance, even though we haven't seen any evidence. How does this happen?

Faith isn't something we can "muster up." It is a gift from God. It's believing God to be faithful to His Word and His promises, even when we don't see anything to prove it. It's saying, "God, I trust You to take care of my problem." Faith is saying you believe before you've seen anything change. It's putting your hope in God.

I love the part in the NWI that says, "will be made fertile and bring forth abundantly." It reminds me of planting seeds. When you plant a seed, you have hope, anticipation, and faith that what you planted in the soil will grow. But how exciting it is when not only do the plants grow, but they produce lots and lots of produce! This verse says that the ground and plants will be made fertile so that they can produce and bring forth abundantly.

In other words, just because you plant seeds doesn't mean you'll be able to get any plants, let alone they produce abundantly. Normally, you have to prepare the soil and continue to weed, fertilize, and so on in order for everything to grow and be healthy. This verse tells us that, because we have put our trust and hope in the Lord, *He* will cause the soil to be fertile and bring forth produce abundantly. Glory to God! Our only role is to trust in the Lord as our Savior and rely on Him for our salvation, health and deliverance. He will bring confidence into us to believe without seeing. When we have this kind of faith Jesus says in John 20:29b "blessed are they that have not seen, and yet have believed."

Father, I come to You believing You and Your Word to be true. I know that, as I pray in Jesus' name, You will hear my prayers. I thank You, Lord, that as I trust You for my answers, You will bless my faith and answer my prayer.

MY REFLECTION:

_____

_____

_____

_____

_____

_____

_____

_____

_____

_____

_____

_____

_____

_____

_____

_____

_____

_____

_____

_____

DAY 99
FORGIVING

JOB 42:10

"And the Lᴏʀᴅ turned the captivity of Job, when he prayed for his friends: also the Lᴏʀᴅ gave Job twice as much as he had before."

"And the self-existent and eternal Lord turned back away and ceased the captivity of Job, the patriarch that was hated as an enemy, when he interceded, prayed for and made supplication for his associates, friends, neighbors and wife: also the Lord added again, and continued to give more, increasing and strengthening Job twice as much, doubling the amount, that he had before." (NWI)

Wow, wow, wow! God can't help but bless Job. Matthew 5:44 says, "But I say unto you, Love your enemies, bless them that curse you, do good to them that hate you, and pray for them which despitefully use you, and persecute you." Luke 6:27-28 says, "But I say unto you which hear, Love your enemies, do good to them which hate you, bless them that curse you, and pray for them which despitefully use you."

Job practiced New Testament commandments from Jesus! He was praying for and essentially blessing those who were putting him down, accusing him of doing something wrong when he hadn't, trying to get him to turn away from God, persecuting him and acting more like his enemies rather than people who were supposed to be his friends. God intervened and let the "friends" know who His favor was upon. He let Job know He had it all under control. Because of this, Job realized more intimately Who God was—not just someone he heard about, but now someone he knew.

Instead of doing what he probably felt like doing before, Job made the decision to forgive, pray for and bless those who had been misunderstanding, critical, judgmental, and hurtful. Job reached down deep and chose to pray for them rather than curse them, because he could understand them through God's eyes. Not only did the Lord give him back what the devil took from him, but this verse says God gave him twice as much (or "double for his trouble," so to speak).

We cannot out-give God. When we are going through difficult times, it can seem like our "captivity" will last forever. Just like Job had to go through all the "steps" of grieving his losses, dealing with people who were *supposed* to have his best interest at heart, and trying to understand what had just happened and why, we need to do the same. But also like Job, we must come to the place where we surrender it all to God. We must realize that though our trial may be more than we think we can bear, God is with us in the middle of the fire, helping us, holding our hand, leading us, and never leaving us. He was faithful to Job and He'll be faithful to us. He will bring us through.

We need to completely rest in and trust Him. As we pray for those who have persecuted us, despitefully used us, and hurt us, He will bring us out of that captive place to the other side of blessing.

> Father, help me bless those who have unrightly judged me
> and hurt me. Show me how to effectively pray for them
> so that not only I, but they also, will be free in You.

MY REFLECTION:

_____

_____

_____

_____

_____

_____

_____

_____

_____

_____

_____

_____

_____

_____

_____

_____

DAY 100
PATIENCE

JAMES 1:3-4

"Knowing this, that the trying of your faith worketh patience. But let patience have her perfect work, that ye may be perfect and entire, wanting nothing."

"Be aware, know, and absolutely be resolved of the fact that the testing or trying because of your conviction of the truthfulness of God, reliance upon Christ, and being constant in your belief accomplishes hopeful endurance, patience and continuance in your waiting. But let continual, hopeful, and enduring patience keep, recover, and accompany your growth, mental, or moral character and acts of labor that you may be perfectly sound in body, whole and complete in every part, not failing, lacking or wanting anything." (NWI)

We never want to go through trials, problems, or difficulties; but unfortunately, they are part of our lives. James learned, and I am learning, that going through those things helps us. It's never fun, but if we can keep our eyes on the Lord instead of what is causing us to "have a bad day," He will not only bring us through it all—He will also build our character.

James tells us that the main thing God does in us when we are going through difficult times is to help us have more patience. Patience helps us to be satisfied and content. It also helps us to grow spiritually, mentally, and morally to become the men and women God has called us to be. In addition, patience makes us "perfect, whole, not lacking or wanting anything". What a promise!

Verse 2 says that we should, "count it all joy when ye fall into temptations." If you read that verse without reading the two verses after it, you may not understand why James makes that statement. It doesn't make any sense whatsoever if you don't include verses 3 and 4. Why would anyone think it joyful to go through temptations? But James understood, and tried to relay to us, that the reason we can be joyful when we're going through temptations. It's because there is a blessing that comes with the trial.

Notice that James never said to count it all joy *for* the temptation. He doesn't say to be a crazy person and be happy for problems. What he is saying is that *when* trials and temptations come (and they will), we can have joy because we know the Lord will use it to perfect us and help us to have patience. Through patience, we will grow to be whole in body, mind and moral character.

Personally, I would rather not have to go through the temptations and trials of life, but I can honestly say that they have all given me a richer perspective and a better understanding of people and things. They have enabled me to develop more compassion, empathy, and understanding—plus I have become less judgmental and critical because I now know what people are going through.

Each experience we encounter gives us a different perspective. For instance, I can read about flying in an airplane and see pictures of one, but it's not the same as seeing them in person or flying in one. I can read about people losing a loved one. I can go to a funeral and see their grieving. But it's not until I personally have lost a loved one that I have the full understanding of how it feels.

So, once again, if I could choose to receive the benefits of going through tribulations without having to actually go through them, I would love that. But just like reading about something gives us a glimpse into what it's like without really allowing us to experience it firsthand, so it is with trials. Is it fun to go through trials and temptations? No! But we need to keep our eyes on the Lord when we are going through them, because He will bring us through and bless us with patience that perfects us.

Lord, thank You for the trials and temptations You have brought
me through. Thank You for helping me grow into the person
You know I can be. Thank You for teaching me patience.

MY REFLECTION:

_____

_____

_____

_____

_____

_____

_____

_____

_____

_____

CPSIA information can be obtained
at www.ICGtesting.com
Printed in the USA
JSHW052347090723
44216JS00002B/20

9 781959 095224